The Intertwined Experience: An Inward Journey in Companionship Building
Part 1 of 2

BY: DANIEL PONCE

1

Acknowledgements:

I would like to thank the following individuals for their contributions in writing this book. I would first like to thank God for continually trying to showing me how to love unconditionally. He has shown me an example of what to strive for. To Dorothy Alberti, who has shown an essence of this love in human form. To my children, who have learned to love me even with all of my deficiencies. To my mother, who has always been that first foundational love I have used as the first cornerstone for all my other relationships. To my father, who strived to teach me many things, including what yearning to be loved felt like. Thanks to Openbookeditors.com for their editing services with this material. Thanks also to ESA/Hubble for the use of their stunning images.

Image for Cover

Book front and back Image cover by-ESA/HUBBLE Images. HUBBLE NICMOS Infrared of M51 as noted in archives as *opo1103b[1]*.

U.S. Patent Pending.

ISBN 978-0-9885409-3-4

Disclaimer

This first of two books will assist the reader in growing aware of those components within themselves. These internal components will guide the reader to greater awareness in how they approach and maintain relationships. By being aware of these internally driven components, we can evaluate them objectively and either keep them if we are comfortable or choose to change them if we are not. This book is not a replacement for professional counseling. If you feel that you are in need of some form of counseling for any relationship issues, please see your therapist, counselor, or any other type of certified trained practitioner, based on your personal needs.

Contents

1. Relationships: Established from Childhood....................7

2. So What is Love— An Objective Perspective.................17

3. Development of One's Gender Identity........................32

4. The Biological Drive..42

5. Attributes of Four Levels of Human Development......52

6. Life's Stages—How to work With Them.......................74

7. The Mirror—Reflections of Your Past........................88

8. Completing the Full Image—Where to now?...............98

Foreword

I am a great liar. I say to myself that I am a perfect companion for my partner. Every day I tell myself that I am fulfilling my part in maintaining the relationship I am in. Internally, I see myself as being loving, generous, patient, and respectful. Ah, but this is my internal perspective as I see myself being in the relationship. This may not be the perception that my partner has of me. She may see me in another light. How can I not see this? Because I am using a subjective mirror to see myself as that perfect companion and not the objective mirror of continually receiving feedback from my companion, family, and acquaintances to help me see myself as I truly am. I must graciously receive their input so that I may change into a better person. That is why I am a great liar. In order to be a great companion for my significant other (as well as for others), I have to be skilled at responding to current experiences based the lessons of past relationships and experiences. This approach to self-improvement has to be based on an internal perspective that I have of myself. Only when I have thoroughly developed these skills will I be able to provide my companion (and others) with her basic and dynamic needs. This is essential to becoming a great companion. As I become a great companion for her, she will also more than likely reciprocate the same level of self-awareness and effort. It all begins with being aware of who you are, your developed skills, and your intention of thriving in a dynamic and powerful relationship.

This book is intended for those people who, like me, desire to become a dynamic life partner, but who aren't quite there yet. With Book 1, I hope to clarify who we are to ourselves and as a companion to our significant other. Through the process of experiencing internal objective reflections, we can begin to develop deeper insights about ourselves so as to become a better partner for our significant other. This includes who we have developed into and what we can offer and ask from our significant others.

May I recommend as you read this material that you begin a personal journal. As you read each chapter, take time to reflect. This reflection should be at times superficial and at other times deep. But it should always be sincere. By journaling and being honest with your thoughts, feelings and past experiences, you can develop greater clarity and truth regarding who you are and how you have become this way. By taking this journey, you will provide yourself with the insight and tools necessary to restructure your thoughts, behavioral patterns, and eventually your personality so as to become a better companion. I would hope that you journal daily, if possible. If not, then at least have a journal handy every time you sit down to read this material.

Relationships: Its Foundation Established from Childhood

What an unparalleled experience—to be in a healthy, loving relationship. The need to connect to someone special is a fundamental drive within the human experience. We are constantly in the process of engaging others by the fundamental need to be a part of something greater than ourselves. In engaging with other people, we talk, understand, and reach out to others to connect with them. For most of us, this seems to be as essential as breathing. We are prodded to begin this dynamic process from youth, which for most of us stems from being in a family structure.

Family structures come in many shapes and sizes. Most of us are given a parental relationship that becomes our essential link to the outside world. They are the individuals whom we will have first developed relationships with. They will set the standard for how we will shape the rest of the relationships in our lives. Of course, our mothers are our focal points of establishing that relationship pattern. Our helpless infant state, in which we are so utterly dependent upon our mothers, allows us to develop the *trust* that we will use later. That trust can lead to developing more powerful forms of emotional and mental attachment, such as being at ease mentally with others and our environment. The mother is the nucleus of all relationships. Without that powerful, supportive, loving, and tender care we learn quickly that the world is not a safe place. A loving, caring, affectionate, patient mother signals us that the world can be a safe and wondrous place to experience. Our mother is the first human intimate contact with the outside world. She provides for us, through the repeated, dynamic and complex interactions with her, the scaffolding by which to build other relationships.

The next major figure that helps most of us develop our ability to form relationships is our father. He sets the stage for developing a new type of dependency. His bonding would be not one of essentiality, but rather one of convenience. His appearance in our lives is usually less physically essential, but no less important. We come to understand that he is part of the surroundings and gradually increases his engagement with us during our infancy. We come to understand that his relationship is a form of a supplemental support system (a back-up system if you will). As infants, we being aware of his presence, can indulge ourselves engaging with him with a somewhat curiosity perspective, based simply on wanting to know more about this person simply by the fact that he is around our immediate environment. We do not have to take any risks with this person, for our mother is close by. With a simple cry, we know that we can be returned to her waiting arms. And so our father really represents our first relationship based on self-indulgence. His presence allows us to explore, engage, and connect with others apart from our mother. In many ways, our bonds with our fathers can be viewed as something having more pure intentions—we engage with him not out of necessity, but simply because we want to. And so our father may represent our first non-essential desire to connect to another person, motivated by a genuine non-essential desire to connect. There may be, however, others around us who are closer to our level of development.

The sibling connection is the next level of engagement in terms of experiencing relationships as infants and toddlers. If we are born into a family with siblings, we have the opportunity to explore our potential for developing relationships by connecting with our siblings which then leads to the formation of another type of relationship. Our sibling connections are not based on authority. Instead we are more likely to be able to relate to our siblings as peers. Our siblings look like us, speak like us, and can act more like us than our parents. We have the opportunity to engage with our siblings on equal footing, rather than from an authoritarian perspective. We engage our siblings with a zest to explore the outside world, and we do this through them. We familiarize ourselves with someone other than ourselves, through how they engage with us and how we respond back to them. We engage with them, exploring through our own ever-increasing curiosity and a desire to connect. They do things that our parents do not do, which can stimulate our curiosity and entertain us. Being the naturally egocentric beings that we are, we tend to see the world from our own perspective. Over time, we come to accept our siblings into our daily experiences and our developing concept of our reality. In time, we bond with them, just as we do with our parents. Depending upon our number of siblings, we gain many opportunities to form lasting, permanent bonds. Some bonds will be stronger than others, depending largely on how much we can communicate and empathize with our siblings. As the years pass, they will teach us much about ourselves. They are uniquely equipped to also show us how best to relate to people and how our parental teachings will be shown through our siblings through their thoughts and behaviors with others.

Through these critical first steps in life, in which we form early bonds with our nuclear family, the stage is set for our escalating ability to form relationships and bonds with other people. The nuclear family has always been, and shall always be, the pillar by which all other relationships will be built. This is the advantage of being raised in a traditional family setting. As the years will pass, we will continue to engage others that will not be part of the core family structure. They will be the extended family such as uncles, aunts and cousins. Even next-door neighbors, many of whom will have children of their own can in time become extended family. Most of us will bond with these neighborhood children. These people from our youth will offer even more opportunities to practice the art of engaging, working, and even enjoying the company of other people later in life.

A great example of having experienced, developed, and having been successful in these early stages of developing relationship with people can be demonstrated by simply asking yourself—do you remember your childhood friends? Perhaps you feel a rush of memories and emotional impressions flooding your mind and heart as you reminisce about childhood friends. This reaction is an example of the bonds that remain from those first years as a child, and how you bonded with children you first played with so long ago.

Recall how your childhood friends made you come alive and allowed you to explore the world while playing, talking, and enjoying the sheer awe of discovery.

Consider if you will what it would be like to not have been provided with a traditional family as the basis of your relationships with others? Consider how you would be like in your relationships with others when you could not have established that first fundamental relationship with your own mother? As mentioned previously, mothers provide the basis by which all relationships will have been established. There are people today, who have such childhood backgrounds. These would include foster children taken from their parents in childhood, children who were reared by distant relatives or children orphaned by family deaths in orphanages, where children were too young to remember their mothers or fathers. A person who doesn't benefit from that first established trust with their biological mother or father during their most vulnerable years of learning can be crippled from having the necessary skills of how to develop healthy dynamic relationships with others.

This possible outcome is commonly argued in Erik Erickson's *Psychosocial Stages of Development*. His position is clearly stated on the crucial window of development for infants: "From warm, responsive care, infants gain a sense of trust, or confidence, that the world is good. Mistrust occurs when infants have to wait too long for comfort and are handled harshly."[1] This established concept that the world is a good place is crucial to building trust in others. If the world treats you well and provides for your needs, it becomes easier to establish trust. In other words, if the world is not hurtful, you can feel safe around others and surpass your hierarchy of basic needs. These basic needs would include food and shelter, as argued by Maslow in his hierarchy of needs. All this can be possible by simply having developed a strong healthy relationship with your mother. If you have not experienced how to first bond with your parents by learning how to

---

[1] Berk, L. (2008). Exploring Lifetime Development. Pg. 13. Boston, MA. Pearson Education, Inc.

established trust, how can you establish any new relationships with others? The concept is clear: trust with your first primary care provider – whether it's your mother, a related family member, or even a foster parent – would have been an essential first step for you. This first ability to establish trust is essential for taking risks, to reach out, and explore the world. The ability to form new relationships falls within this process.

Many women have raised their children with the ideas and rules they inherited from their own mothers. This background experience, based on having only one type of exposure to maternal training is a fact of human experience. This fact can have both positive and negative qualities to it. On one hand, a new mother drawing from the experiences she had with her own mother will use this limited resource to draw from when she finds herself with a newborn child. On the other hand, a woman benefits from at least some form of training in rearing their young by having seen their own mothers engage their younger siblings, for example. The specifics of how a new mother rears her children can greatly vary from one family to another. However, culture, ethnicity, socioeconomic status, heritage, family traditions, and many other factors play into this process of motherly training, each child-rearing experience is unique. Having pointed out that one's life experience is based on one's own unique set of circumstances, it's important to consider the outcome of engaging the world with the particular form of parental training you have inherited. This is an interesting question worth exploring.

There are many outcomes to each unique style and form of child-rearing one can have experienced. Each unique background setting will also contribute towards your developed approach in developing relationships. So what are some of these effects to the various forms of child-rearing? If you were a person who had a mother of uncompromised maternal qualities, it's clear that good fortune has befallen you! You were taught early in life that the world is safe, secure, and trustworthy. You may even have been encouraged to explore the world around you by later in life being prone to travel, experiencing new cultures and new types of people. You will possess the confidence to take many risks in life.

Another possible outcome would be having a strict or demanding mother. The outcome of this style of mothering would more than likely have you instilled to expect or demand much from yourself as well as from others. Your willingness to engage the world may become compromised by your own impatience and strict expectations of others. Your rules of conduct for yourself and others will likely be rigid. If your mother was harsh, you will have learned quickly that the world is indeed a harsh place, where trust will be a hard component to find. You may have developed little trust for other people. Other peoples' motives will always being questioned. Patience may be a precious commodity in your life as well. If your mother was neglectful to you as a child, you will have learned very little about your own unique qualities and attributes and will struggle in appreciating the greatness that lies within you. You may also find yourself struggling to hold relationships with other people due to your lack of self-esteem and self-acceptance. There are so many other types and combinations of experiences possible in your childhood. These potential different experiences that your mother will have potentially played in your life will have impressed upon you what you will consider to be *normal* for the rest of your life. If you find that you can see an unacceptable pattern of you dealing with others then perhaps counseling with a trained therapist may be just the thing for you. More on this topic later. Your pattern of behavior will also play out differently depending on your gender.

Ingrained patterns of thought and behavior tend to repeat themselves in relationships. If you were a male who benefitted from a strong maternal figure, you will more than likely seek out women that will possess these same motherly attributes. Women who lack these attributes will more than likely be shunned by the male, depending upon his level of personal development. As a woman who had a strong maternal figure, you will likely also display these motherly attributes to the men you encounter. On the other hand, a male who had a weak maternal figure as a child will tend to be drawn to women who have other attributes that your mother did not display. As a woman with a similar childhood experience, you will likely seek out older maternal figures that will display behavior that you would prefer being reflected in yourself. If you are not aware that these were negative experiences, you will likely display these same attributes to your potential mate.

It's important to consider the paternal figure as well. The effects of being exposed to a strong paternal figure will impact how you deal with authority figures in your future. If your father figure was patient and loving, you are indeed fortunate. In life, you will understand that through this type of exposure, the continual experiences in life of dealing with authority (in its myriad of forms) will be accepted with patience, respect, and understanding. If, on the other hand, your fatherly figure was impatient, unforgiving, and harsh, you will likely be fighting authority for much of your life. As a male with favorable fatherly-child interactions, you will assume the attributes of your father due to the strong admiration you will have acquired for him during your childhood. As a woman also with a positive male role model, more than likely you will seek out men with similar attributes as your father. If there was no fatherly figure in your childhood, the role of a father will likely remain a confusing concept for you. You may also find yourself fighting authority time after time, or perhaps with counseling learn to become comfortable with it. Another interesting outcome of childhood where both parents took care of you and one of the two parents had aversive engagements with you is also possible. One possible outcome could be where your father was loving but your mother was harsh. A girl with this background would later tend to have more male friends than female friends. Conversely, a male with a gentle mother and a harsh father will likely tend to prefer the company of women. Again, there are also many other types of experiences that are possible with your first authority figures.

The relationships you developed with your siblings may be one that will affect the relationships you will have with your peers later in life. How will you get along with those people that have more in common with you just as you had more in common with your siblings as a child? Your siblings will play an integral part of how you will be engaging your friends, classmates, associates at work, and other individuals in your age group. Were you and your siblings play-partners? Did you confide in each other? Conversely, perhaps you and your siblings were constantly challenging each other, trying to outdo one another. Or did you always find yourself fighting with them? As you did with your siblings, more than likely you will be doing with your peers. Consider what it would be like to not have any siblings? There are many people who have this childhood background as a part of their childhood experiences. From these varying precarious childhood experiences just mentioned, getting along with your peers may be a mystery, for you may not know how to properly engage them and maintain healthy relationships with them. This is often true for children who were in constantly in strife with their siblings as a child.

As an only child, you likely get along well with authority figures today due to your good relationships with your parents. You may, however, struggle to get along with your peers due to the lack of relationship building you were not afforded in childhood. As an only child, having benefitted from the full amount of resources provided to you by your parents (attention, education, emotional support, financial resources, etc.), you will likely excel in your verbal abilities and become a strong student in the classroom. Getting along with your peers may become a deep lesson for you to learn, however, due to your decreased need to bond to the peers around you.

So are we locked into our experiences based solely on how we got along with our family? Absolutely not. There are always opportunities to engage others in many different ways. There is a cornucopia of types of people in the world. Each person is unique; with a unique set of experiences, abilities, and perspectives. Engaging with a variety of other people with different cultures, ethnicities, values and belief systems provides a wealth of opportunities to grow and expand your understanding of the many facets of human potential. By engaging with people different than you, you can expand your repertoire of social experiences. You can develop new strategies of engaging with people, learn from other's experiences, and even expand your ability to cultivate relationships with different types of people. While learning from others, you may uncover the opportunity to develop a profile of what attributes you would like to have and begin to re-train yourself into the type of person you want to be. We are often attracted to others because they possess traits and qualities that we wish we possessed. But first, we must know who we want to become in order to know what we can become. This is true for ourselves as well as for our chosen companion. We will eventually discuss this concept in depth in another chapter.

Our ability to be a good companion is based strongly on the fact that we first learned about relationships during the days when we were crawling around on the floor, attempting to speak words that were unclear to our parents and we were exploring everything around us, often by putting many objects into our mouths. Our parents were, and shall always be, the original architects of our ability to develop relationships with others. Our siblings also provided an additional opportunity to expand this process of forming relationships. Our grandparents, uncles, aunts, and cousins often provide us with further opportunities to develop our ability to establish and build relationships.

If you find yourself in a fulfilling relationship, many congratulations to you! However, if you often find yourself in heated debates with others or unable to get along well with your companion, perhaps it is time to direct your energy and efforts toward developing better strategies to promote healthier relationships. Healthier relationships foster opportunities to grow and develop. It is only through building relationships that friendships are made, companions are found, business engagements are struck, and opportunities appear. However, this only happens if you can simply take time to redirect your method of engaging others based on being genuine sharing of yourself, and motivated by the idea that you are interested in getting to know your potential partner for who they are.

You are not alone in your risk-taking actions. Perhaps you do not have many friends and desire to make more. If you find yourself in this situation, being honest with how you engage people may provide the insight necessary to redirect your thoughts and behaviors to more acceptable methods of engaging people. Perhaps the time has arrived to receive counseling from a trained therapist, who can teach you how to objectively look at how you engage people and gently recommend another approach to try. These specialists are trained in identifying both healthy and unhealthy behavioral patterns. You are in good hands when you confide in these professionals of human relationships. However, it is important to always remember that the origins of how you approach relationship building first began with your parents.

This childhood background experience is the beginning coursework of training for all of us in developing relationships. This includes engagement in a variety of relationships under many types of conditions such as work, home, social clubs, etc. It is through our childhood experiences that we have been trained on how to get along with others. Through the years we have either refined those strategies or resisted them by recognizing that perhaps they could be improved by simply choosing to reprogram ourselves. Being cognizant of this simple fact can offer us the ability to empower ourselves to be in healthier relationships.

Do you think you need to change your approach when engaging others? Do you feel that you need to change certain things about yourself? Are you satisfied with your current relationships? This cognizant mental state is a healthy first step in reforming yourself, to be aware of how you have been trained and how to deal with people. From this fundamental perspective, we can begin to change how we approach others so that we can become a better companion for our significant other for now and for our future.

So What is Love—An Objective Perspective

Love. What a profound four-letter word. Regardless of the era researched, the subject of love will always be found written within the most profound and memorable passages of history. Love can be a simple misused word, such as loving a piece of chocolate cake or loving how one's new power-tool works. Conversely, it can be a profound human expression between two people. It can also be a powerful spiritual concept, as has been discussed in holy passages discussed in books about the virtues of divine being. It can bring you to great heights with its acquirements or to tremendous lows with its loss. Wars have been fought to preserve it. Love has also prevented wars from starting. Anyone who has experienced its profound grasp is forever changed by it. It can transform you into someone you did not know you could become. As to what love truly is remains a mystery. There is no clear explanation of what this most profound experience is. This deep expression of human potential has been studied objectively in the scientific community. It has provided us some insights as to how the experience of love changes and affects us physically and mentally as well as emotionally as it plays itself out in our lives.

Psychologists can quantify the process of experiencing love through empirical research (the approach of studying some given phenomenon by the collection of data from an observed event). Through a variety of empirical approaches, psychologists have observed people in a variety of situations and collected data that has been used to discuss their unique life experiences with this subject of love, all in the hope of developing patterns and reaching objective conclusions. Psychologists can objectively gauge people's attitudes and behaviors with love and measure some anatomical and physiological processes that the body and mind experiences while in this state of being in love. Through these types of approaches, psychologists have objectively analyzed the process of love and have come to some surprising conclusions of how love affects our bodies and mind.

Some psychologists have theorized that there are many forms of love. Other researchers suggest that love has one core feature that can be seen in a variety of relationships. Of the many concepts developed about love, the work of John Lee (1977) has been considered a great step forward in objectively understanding what love is. Lee in his theory of love has categorized six major types of love:[2]

- Eros—erotic desire for an idealized person, such as a romantic or passionate love-as is seen in the beginning of a new relationship.

- Ludus—playful or game-like love in which a person can have multiple partners. Here, the person with multiple partners will manipulate or play with their partners so as to obtain complete control over them with the intention of dominating them.

- Storge—slowly developing an attachment to someone over a period of time. Here, the two people spending time together begin to form an attachment based on mutual affection that will grow over time. In this setting, friendship is first established, followed by romantic encounters.

- Mania—obsessive and jealous love in which the act of being in love with someone is similar to experiencing a life-changing event. Here, the person experiencing this form of love loses themselves in the process of being infatuated with the other person. Here, love can appear as an impulsive and obsessive act.

---

[2]. http://valarie-king.hubpages.com/hub/Understanding-Different-Types-of-Lovers.

- Agape—altruistic love or expressing love for another based on care for the other person, similar to how a parent nurtures a child.

- Pragma—practical love, in which a person experiencing this form of love will use reasoning and logic to make decisions about their partner instead of passion or desire. Here, they logically weigh the pros and cons of entering into a relationship with their partner.

All of these expressions of love can be easily confused one with another where one type can appear like another. For example, the Storge type of love, which is a slow developing bond, can be mistaken for the Pragma form of love, which is the unification of people from common goals and interests. Another example is Eros, which is a physical love induced by the chemistry of attraction for the opposite sex, which can be confused with Ludis, which is an expression of love as if excited for the other person, in a constant game of on-off behaviors. I would suggest that each person can experience two or even three types of these forms of love at once. If we simply take the time to reflect upon our own experiences of having been in love, we can distinguish which forms of love we have experienced or are currently experiencing. We can also come to understand that the act of love can graduate from one form to another (i.e. from Ludus to Storge to Agape) while possibly still maintaining some elements of a previous form of love.

In an analytic study conducted in 1984, Robert Sternberg and Susan Gracek identified one strong connection which interrelates the various forms of love—the ability for partners to communicate effectively and share and support one another. Today, we call this process intimacy.[3] So what is intimacy?

---

[3] Cohen, L. (Feb. 2011). The Psychology of Love. Psychology Today. Retrieved from: http://www.psychologytoday.com/blog/handy-psychology-answers/201102/the-psychology-love

Ronald Adler and Russell Proctor II discuss four ways by which people can feel connected to a chosen partner. These four dimensions of intimacy include:

- "Physical – Hugging, kissing, caressing, cuddling, holding, and other forms of physical affection. Physical intimacy certainly includes sexual intercourse but doesn't have to. As long as other aspects of the relationship remain sound, physical intimacy between partners can often last a lifetime, even if sexual potency diminishes due to factors such as health, age, and stress.

- Emotional – The ability to effectively express and validate tender, loving emotions, in a manner that's nourishing and constructive, and being able to respond affirmatively when the other person does the same. Examples include: "How are you doing?" "How are you feeling?" "I love you," "I appreciate you," "I like it when we talk like this," "You're very important in my life," and "I'm sorry."

- Intellectual – Can brains be attractive and sexy? Absolutely. Especially for those who feel a sense of kinship when they engage in discussions or endeavors with a partner whom they feel is an intellectual equal.

- Shared Activities – Interactions that build a positive memory bank of shared experiences. Examples include playing, cooking, dancing, exercising, art making, traveling, worshipping, and problem solving together. In this dimension, it's not just the activity that matters, but whether two people are able to bond while interacting with one another."[4]

[4] Ni, P. (Sept., 2012), *How to enhance closeness in your relationship*. Psychology Today. Retrieved from: http://www.psychologytoday.com/blog/communication-success/201209/how-enhance-closeness-in-your-relationship

These four levels of connecting with a companion are considered the main type of interactions through which we can express our needs and wants. Our partner, once they see us practicing these types of approaches to intimacy, may begin to reciprocate their needs and wants with us in a similar manner. Through these various forms of intimacy, we stay in more personal and intimate communication with our partners. Let us now turn to the process of how love affects both the anatomical (the physical components) and physiological processes (how these structures work by themselves as well as with each other) in the human body.

A medical approach to what the mind and body goes through as the person develops from an initial stage of infatuation to having developed a lifetime commitment for their chosen partner can be found in the work of Dr. Robert Sternberg, who developed the "Triangular Theory of Love". He theorized that all forms of love consist of three elements: passion (which can be compared to lust), intimacy (which can loosely associated with the concept of attraction) and commitment (which can be associated with attachment).[5] As one's experience of loving someone transforms, the body goes through various phases of physiological *shifting* (adjusting from one responsive aspect of the effects of love to another). At the same time, the mind willingly shifts from one form of love to another, in order to provide the person experiencing a particular type of love with the continued opportunity to nurture and maintain that relationship. The "Triangular Theory of Love" indicates that the potential long-term courtship of a partner begins with passion and leads to intimacy, before finally maturing into commitment.

The concept of passion is defined by a medical dictionary as "great emotion or zeal; frequently associated with sexual excitement."[6] With this initial onset of passion can

---

[5] Cohen, L. (2011). The Psychology of Love. Retrieved from:
http://www.psychologytoday.com/blog/handy-psychology-answers/201102/the-psychology-love
[6] Thomas, C., Editor (1993). Taber's Cyclopedic Medical Dictionary. Philidelphia, PA., F.A. Davis Company.

also arise a psychological arousal of the mind and a euphoric state of the body. In addition to the onset of passion often there comes an unspoken but clearly evident primitive physical drive to be sexually aroused and a desire to be intimacy with the person whom you have become captivated with. With the onset of passion often comes a neuro-physiological connection. This connection – in which the central nervous system, once it becomes aware that a physical attraction has been established – begins releasing hormones to accommodate the mental and physiological state of the body so, as to adapt to this new experienced level of love. These hormones are chemical messages created from one part of the body (the brain in this case) to affect another part of the body. In the case of experiencing love, hormones directed by the brain instruct the tissue being signaled to perform a specific task within the body, according to which stage of love one is in. TI would offer that there are three stages of love (previously attributed to Dr. Sternberg's "Triangular Theory of Love") that allows the body to shift from one form of love to another. This shift can be associated with the various hormones directing the process of each of these stages.[7] The previously mentioned three stages are lust (passion), attraction (intimacy), and attachment (commitment).

The first stage of lust is characterized by the release of testosterone in the male body, or estrogen in the female body. Let us discuss these hormones briefly. Testosterone is a powerful male hormone made in the testes. Testosterone promotes the various secondary characteristics of a man's body. These physical characteristics include: generally being taller in stature than a female, having more upper body strength, growing facial hair, having a deeper voice which signals the presence of testosterone in his body, the development of male genitalia, often demonstrating aggressive behavior, as well as the production and distribution of sperm, as developed in the testes.

---

[7] Author unknown Publication date unknown), The Science of Love. Retrieved from: http://www.youramazingbrain.org/lovesex/sciencelove.htm

The female hormone estrogen provides women with the secondary sexual characteristics, such as; different distribution of fat on her body to emphasize a larger bottom, wider hips, and developed breasts. Other female characteristics include possessing fuller lips, a higher voice to denote the presence of estrogen, and a tendency for having a more nurturing disposition. Testosterone and estrogen work to maintain the manly and womanly features of the human body, so as to promote the opportunity to reproduce. Once a male sees a woman demonstrating the right set of physical biological qualities that informs him that she is capable of reproduction and demonstrates optimal physical features, the testosterone begins to focus the his attention to optimize opportunities with the female. However, the female, being driven by the estrogen hormone, does not have the constant drive of the male body to reproduce. Rather, the woman's drive comes in cyclical patterns, according to her ovulatory cycle. The release of her egg from her ovary into her reproductive tract coincides with a spike in her testosterone levels to promote sexual arousal. This peak in sexual arousal provides the opportunity for fertilization of her egg to occur.

Let us now return to the three phases of love and their associated physiological states as dictated by the hormones which govern the body's reaction. The three stages are:

Stage 1: Lust (can also be termed passion)—As previously mentioned, in this stage, the person is driven by the sex hormones testosterone and estrogen. Here, the body is focused on the person of interest and one having advertised as possessing optimal biological reproductive capacity.

Stage 2: Attraction (can also be termed intimacy). Scientists believe three main neuro-chemicals are dramatically affecting this stage of the love experience: adrenaline/cortisol, dopamine, and serotonin:

- Adrenaline—This initial stage of being infatuated with someone can increase stress levels in your body, which in turn can cause an increase of the hormones adrenalin and cortisol. Adrenaline is the fight-versus-flight hormone that is released from the adrenal glands (glands located just above the kidneys). When released into your bloodstream, your mind and body perceives you to be in peril. Here you either engage the threat with bodily reactions (fight) or run to safety (flight). Cortisol is the hormone that is released every morning at approximately 7:00 a.m. from the pituitary gland in your brain. It can be considered your shot of morning coffee to start the day off. The brain can also increase cortisol levels when it perceives stress. Both hormones maintain a continued mental vigilance for the person you have become infatuated with. It helps you stay focused with your targeted person of interest.

- Dopamine—This hormone originates in the ventral tegmental area of the brain (deep within the brain). This area of the brain sends this hormone to another area of the brain called the nucleus accumbens area (also found centrally located in the brain). Dopamine stimulates the experience of desire by triggering intense rushes of pleasure and good feelings. It is known that while in this state, couples have shown an increase in energy, less need for sleep, and less desire to eat. Dopamine also promotes a more focused attention onto the person of their interest.

- Serotonin—This hormone is known to generally stimulate routine brain activity, this hormone in increased levels in the brain is believed to be the hormone that influences you to obsess over the person you desire. Serotonin is also known to contribute to the ability of the Central Nervous System (CNS) to regulate mood, sleep, and appetite, along with memory and learning. In an experimental study done by Dr. Donatella Marazziti in Pisa, Italy, it was discovered that in the early phase of love (the attraction phase), changes occur to how you process information.[8] For her study, she recruited twenty couples who had been recently caught by the intensity of love for a period of less than six months. She took blood samples and checked the serotonin levels, comparing them to other people known to suffer from Obsessive-Compulsive Disorders (a mental state where your mind repeatedly focuses in on one single thought for extended periods of time). The study concluded that the serotonin levels were similar. Thus, this study found that serotonin can contribute to an obsessive phase of love that is commonly experienced when you are deep within love's early stages.

Stage 3: Attachment (also be termed commitment)—this final and most mature phase of love is believed to be made possible in part by two hormones. These hormones are oxytocin and vasopressin.

- Oxytocin is released by the pituitary gland of the brain when the mother hears the newborn crying. When released, milk is quickly discharged from the mother's lacrimal ductal glands of the breast to meet the need of the newborn's desire to feed. A powerful emotional attachment is also made by oxytocin's effects on the mother's brain for the newborn as well. Oxytocin is also known to be released during the intimate act of an orgasm as new couples will tend to have frequent sexual encounters as the first weeks and months pass together.

- Vasopressin (also released from the pituitary gland) is normally released to assist the body in regulating the water levels in the blood, especially as the kidney filters the blood. Vasopressin is another important hormone that is released after the act of sex. It is unclear as to

---

[8] Author unknown Publication date unknown), The Science of Love. Retrieved from: http://www.youramazingbrain.org/lovesex/sciencelove.htm

what function this hormone plays in the process of developing an attachment, but it is speculated that this hormone promotes attachment over time. Therefore, it can be argued that with newer couples having sex more frequently, as is commonly seen early in relationships, the more of these two hormones are released. This continues to bond partners together, which eventually can lead to the commitment phase of love.

Depending upon which stage you are in, be it either the lust stage (regulated by the hormones of testosterone or estrogen), attraction stage (regulated by adrenaline/cortisol as well as dopamine and serotonin), or the attachment phase (regulated by oxytocin and vasopressin), your mind is sending your body hormones to respond to either an initial biological drive to reproduce – continuing to invest your energy and time into your newly chosen partner – or continuing to maintain this relationship that may have started years ago, but now has developed and blossomed into a complex, dynamic engagement with your chosen partner.

Does this discovered scientific understanding completely encapsulate the concept of love by looking at it from a neurological, anatomical, and physiological perspective? Absolutely not. Although the human body is essential to the human condition, we are much more than just our human body and mind. Within the human mind lives the ability to experience life through the process of emotions. Our emotional ability is as essential to our human experience as our body and mind are. There is a considerable discussion regarding how emotions work and how they play a vital informational role through the emotional filtering mechanism found within the brain. This emotional essential role in guiding the human experience in my book entitled *MY DEEP Training: An Uncommon Guide Toward Spiritual Growth and General Well Being,* which can be found on my website: www.mydeept.com.

To briefly discuss this point, the brain is designed to process information through a filtering mechanism—the emotional capacity of the mind. This emotional capacity can be found in the hippocampus/amygdala area of the limbic system in the brain (in the center of the brain). When experiencing something new, the brain processes this new information through the amygdala which processes the information as being relevant, irrelevant, and the degree of relevance this new experience has related to survival. The amygdala then imprints this processed information with a signaling system, which attaches to the processed experience a unique qualitative message of the degree of relevance the experience has to survival. This processed information has an increased value, a decreased value, or no value at all to help one survive.

We can consider emotions as a method for the brain to enhance the quality of the information gained from an experience. Examples of imprinted information from processed previous experiences include how you *feel* about your mother or father when you think of them. People generally have strong emotions associated with their parents. Other bits of information containing some level of value would be something like your thoughts on politics or about your favorite sports team. Information with no emotional value might include thinking about the number seven or the fact that you are currently are reading a book—this has little or no emotional value associated with it.

Along with experiences containing an emotional attachment is the idea that there is a hierarchical structure to emotions. Emotions can be thought of as possessing either constructive (positive) or destructive (negative) attributes to them. Examples of positive emotions would include experiencing love, joy, and jubilation. Examples of negative emotions would include experiencing anger, rage, or fear. Emotions such as anger or fear are known to be deeply-rooted emotional responses in an animal's brain. Just like as with human, an animal's brain has an innate ability to be able to process experiences by *tagging* them with a variety of emotional responses. The amygdala is also the area known to harbor the higher aspects of emotions, such as the ability to want to laugh, feel happiness, and even more complex emotion such as love.

I would offer that it is possible for emotions to be an expressive outlet of what may be happening deep within the regions of the mind versus simply being a tagging system to measure the relative degree of some experience. When you consider that we process information about some event that occurred or a memory of some event that occurred, we are responding to this experience by producing an emotional response. This attaches a qualitative value – either positive (such as feeling joy from the experience or thought) or a negative value (such as becoming angry from the experience or memory of it). It is not clear, however, through the study of neuroscience whether the processed information in the human brain chooses to respond to an event by forming an emotion *after* it has processed it, or tagging an emotional response *during* the state of processing the information. If the brain creates the emotional response after it processes the information, it must then be telling the amygdala to label the experience with an either positive or negative state based on a developed value system within the brain. If the human brain begins to process information of some experience, while it is processing this information, it will formulate either a negative or positive response to the processed information. Thus, the amygdala is a minimal player in the labeling of information. If it is possible that the amygdala is playing a minimal role in the labeling of emotions, it becomes clear that emotional content is found throughout the complexity of the brain and not simply localized to the area of the amygdala. Therefore, the ability to experience the higher aspects of emotions, such as humor, epiphanies, and jubilation, are possible only for the most developed animal brains in the animal kingdom, according to their state of complexity in design.

Within this group of highly developed animals are whales, elephants, dolphins and, of course, humans. This ability of higher life forms to experience higher states of emotions raises a question: to what end does it serve a human being to experience higher states of emotion, such as love or happiness? It is clear that in referring to the human condition, the emotion of love can profoundly alter a person's psychological state as previously explained. This ability of love to affect the psychological state must therefore be also able to affect the neurological structure of the brain. Therefore, I would speculate that even though we can see the effects of hormones as found during changes in physiological functions and neurological behaviors, it may be possible that hormones are the byproducts of changes to the human brain and to the human mind, according to the brain's need to survive.

For example, when the brain experiences love, this in turn creates hormones, rather than hormones being created by the physiological and anatomical changes seen in the human brain and body. I would offer that the experience of love includes more than physiological changes in the body. The act of experiencing love involves a higher ability of the human brain. When experiencing love, we are able to access a higher state of awareness to ourselves, the person we love, and the world around us in general. We also gain new insights into the world around us by going through this process. Through this higher state of awareness, we are afforded a key to open up the higher aspects to ourselves and to our reality. From this most influential of experiences, we open up other aspects of our lives that have long been dormant. This includes committing ourselves to our loved ones and other virtues, such as putting others before you, giving without expecting anything in return, and being able to be aware of other gifts, such as developing a more spiritual state of existence.

Cosmologists (scientists that study the structure and function of the universe) tell us that the universe is known to be vast, expansive, complicated, and mysterious. The universe has many properties such as cosmic events being cyclical, energetic, as well as matter and energy being two sides of the same coin. The universe having many unknown patterns of behavior yet to be determined by the scientific community possesses as yet many unknown properties. One property in particular about the universe is the fact that the universe once had a beginning (according to our current understanding). If the universe had a beginning, there must be some force which initiated this process. The nature of this force or we call this force a Creator, can be understood by studying the characteristics of its creation similar to a painting and his painting. As we reflect upon the ideas of the characteristics of the creation, we see the following properties: a seemingly endless event (the universe flowing through her endless activities), vast expansiveness of distance, unimagined foresight in design to the universe, a creative nature, and a presence of love found among its sentient creations (such as us humans). If love can be found among its creation, this Creator himself must also possess some quality of love but at a much higher form. When this Creator expresses himself through love, this love must be expressed by being found interwoven within the fabric of all things created. This interwoven property of love must be found in all of creation, waiting for the right conditions to be manifested. An example of this can be seen with the right set of conditions within the human experience such as a man and a woman coming together to promote their love for one another. It stands to reason that love is not a uniquely human experience. Instead it is a universal phenomenon that refers back to its source—the Creator. Therefore, it is conceivable that love is a unique component found in the universe and is also found within the fabric of all things created. So you see that love is something vastly greater than just some hormones being released by the brain to change the physiological qualities to the body. Its manifestation within the human experience must, therefore, be an essential component of being human, so as to provide a supportive environment to promote human potential, growth, and development.

As we have discussed the basics of love from psychological perspectives to physiological processes, and to even the cosmic level of existence, love must therefore have a maturing aspect. The mysteries of experiencing and being in love appear to be unique to the human condition as ascertained from a human perspective. One thing can be said for sure about love—it will forever change you once you experience it. It will transform you into someone who possesses a greater awareness and an enriched quality of life. Having experienced love, living will take on greater value, and you will have a greater appreciation for it. Being with your partner will have no equal in the world. Everything seems to be in harmony when this occurs, and why not? Love has an inexplicable power over us, awakening within us undiscovered potential and greatness. Lastly, we offer our chosen partner the opportunity to grow with us through this incredible experience. Through love we can acquire a deep appreciation of the virtuous nature of the cosmos itself. The concept of love has always, and will always, lie beyond the reach of the scientific community, for science has not matured sufficiently to be able to grasp the more profound qualities and nature of love.

Development of One's Gender Identity

I am a male. I have come to understand what this means after many years of living within the perception of being a male. I am the product of genetics, society, culture, the influence of my family, and, of course, personal choices. This has allowed me to be raised with certain acquired traits, selective experiences, environmental influences, and other factors that have shaped my interpretation of what a male should be. If I were born female, I could make the same argument of how I have come to develop my female concept of being a woman through another set of unique influences.

As a male, one will begin to explore ideas of sexual activities from the early pre-pubescent years, during which we first become curious about our body, and later the female body. This leads to sexual activities in the late teens, and eventually developing a constant sex drive that lasts well into one's forties, fifties, and beyond. The disproportionate amount of testosterone coursing through a young man's blood inclines him to demonstrate a high state of aggression and a higher degree of showmanship to advertise his various attributes. This goes hand-in-hand with demonstrating, among many of the different attributes of a woman, a muscular body with more upper body strength to complement it. These behaviors will help him attract and court any female that may be attracted to his inherited physical traits. A boy's wet dreams (semenarche) during his pre-teen years, signals to him that his body can produce sperm. A developing young man often turns to his father figure for guidance to help further develop his masculinity as he negotiates his way through puberty.

For a female, the higher existing state of emotional capacity residing within provides her with the ability to become aware of a world full of enriched emotions. By practicing these strong emotional abilities such as having strong attachments and expressing her emotions to her family, peers, and friends, she develops a wealth of emotional content. A developing young lady would also begin to become aware of her sexual impulses by beginning to see boys as attractive, often before any boy recognizes her as attractive. Due to the high degree of estrogen flowing through her pubescence body, the onset of her first menstruation signals her that her body is capable of reproducing. The onset of this dramatic physiological process can bring a young female into an acute state of duress if not properly prepared by her mother or close female relative. The high amount of estrogen flowing through her body would also transform her body to develop breasts, increasingly curvy hips, and other features that will make her uniquely female. She will usually turn to her mother as a guide to teach her about her femininity as well. The woman will have the ability to demonstrate her physical attributes to a male of her choosing so as to provide her the opportunity to create children. These are the normal outcomes to the developing female body as she travels through puberty.

Contrary to a man's biological instincts, in which aggressive behavior is often common, social judicial influences (the law) will tell him what is and is not acceptable behavior. A man can only demonstrate his sexual prowess without breaking the law. The judicial system will not tolerate a male coercing his will upon another person's rights without their approved consent. Society generally expects the male not to show excessive displays of emotion. The male will be expected to be strong in both physical and mental attributes. Society will want to show the male how to be responsible so as to be a good future provider in the years to come. On the other hand, culture encourages the male to act within certain acceptable standards of behavior with family members, acquaintances, and other members of society. Also, depending upon the cultural influence he has been born into, he will either show women the upmost respect or completely show no remorse for treating them as a family member with no rights or privileges. Lastly, family influences can have the upmost influence on a male as well. Depending upon what the mother and father's own inherited set of teachings, they will show the male child their own set of standards about respect, dignity, care, compassion, and other virtues. A male child can certainly be raised to respect himself, his siblings, his parents, other family members, and anyone outside the family. On the other hand, he may develop a complete selfishness, in which he's unable to empathize with anyone except himself. Of course, there is so much in between the two extremes which is where most men fall.

A woman has her own unique share of influences as well. Taking into consideration the similar type of settings that a male will have been exposed to, a woman would have a very different set of influences under these same conditions. Her biological inheritance shapes her body to be groomed for bearing and nurturing children. Her biology grants her the ability to create life; something that no male can ever accomplish. Along with this tremendous ability comes the genetic capacity to be nurturing, loving, and patient among many other attributes that women possess. Most women need these qualities in order to become a nurturing provider for her children and maintain a family structure. These endowed abilities also provide a woman a quality that cannot be matched by any living male—a higher level of emotional content.

The ability to create life and the enhanced emotional states that a woman possesses make her very different from most men. With these two strong genetic influences as a basis to begin her life as a female, and having many similar environmental settings as a male, she will be exposed to a society that will treat her differently based largely on those capacities. Society will tell her that it will be acceptable to cry, hold hands, and generally display her emotions and nurturing skills. In society it is often more acceptable for women to discuss feelings than her male counterparts. It seems that society understands the tremendous harnessed qualities women possess just beneath the surface. Society has a high regard for her ability to bear and rear children, and serve the role of peacemaker and nurturer in society. Then again, if a woman were to break the law, she would be treated with more spitefulness by the judicial system due to the fact that society tends to hold women to a a higher behavioral standard than a man.

Culture also plays an important part in determining who she must become. Depending upon her cultural exposure, she might be looked upon as a person of high standing within society – as is the case in many Native Americans tribes – or simply a vessel to bear children and maintain a household as can be seen being practiced in other parts of the world. Lastly, her family structure will also have a great influence upon her self-concept. She could have been groomed to be strong and responsible by her family. She could also be taught to believe that she is inferior then men. Of course, all families are different. Some families will entrust women to be the primary caretaker of the house, with a variety of important responsibilities. Others will cherish a young lady's virginity and strive to protect the family's dignity in proportion to the young daughter's ability to maintain it prior to marriage. Other families will not treat the daughter any different than the son, and she will be equally encouraged to explore her academic, athletic, and sexual potential to their full extent. Again, you will see everything in between these extremes.

Through the many years of influence, and at times being forced to accept the ways of the world, the boy becomes a man and the girl becomes a woman. They are conditioned to develop and respond to the world and experiences around them so as to become the people they are expected to be. This is an important part of how we become the men and women we see ourselves today, based on the influences and experiences of our pasts. It has been said that each gender has the right to develop and express their own concept of what masculinity is for a man and what femininity is for a woman. Seeing that men and women are groomed to become different types of people in society, occasionally some men and women can develop certain intolerances for the ways of the opposite sex. Thus, an unfavorable polarizing of viewing for the opposite sex can develop.

Have you ever met a man who looked down upon women? How about a woman who had few good things to say about men? There are certainly men and women who develop an unhealthy attitude toward the opposite sex. This unhealthy predisposition can only lead them to unhealthy inner states of imbalance and limit their chances of developing relationships with the opposite sex. In some cases, men harbor bad feelings toward women, perhaps because they have been taken advantage of or used as a financial resource, or even as a means acquiring status among her peers. Other reasons may include the man not having been taught how to show respect for the powerful attributes that a woman possesses. In addition, a man may have been raised to consider women to simply be an object of sexual pleasure, and grow frustrated when they find that women don't respond to his advances. There are so many other reasons why a male would develop a poor concept for women.

From these unhealthy predispositions, a man might develop a mistrust or even a strong distaste for women in general. This male individual, in time, would have few good things to say about women. His ability to maintain a healthy and equal relationship with a woman would be reduced to continuous antagonistic feelings, resulting in behaviors such as arguing, fighting, or a lack of wanting to be around female company in general. If you find yourself demonstrating behaviors like this, it's important to consider these anti-social behaviors to be a warning sign. Much grief and suffering awaits you.

A woman can easily develop mistrust for a male's intentions. Women have been experiencing this problem since the beginning of their ability to enter relationships with men. This mistrust for a male's motives comes from a fundamental drive men have always exhibited towards women—the sheer drive to engage in *sex*. Sex is a powerful biological drive. As a woman develops a strong biological drive to have children, the same thing happens to men. However, unlike the woman, a young male usually does not desire the consequential outcome from the act of sex—creating a child. There is also another strong component to this mistrust—an invested emotional content by the female.

Objectively speaking, women can be compared to emotional juggernauts. Men do not have this capacity. Women develop a powerful capacity for having and expressing emotions. This is an ability that men generally lack. Allow me to provide for you an example of this fact. A female teenager who sees the world through an emotional perspective, cannot begin to be understood by a teenage boy emotionally. Most young girls at this age remain a mystery of expressing emotions. This includes wanting to touch, caress, and hug, and speaking words such as "I care for you deeply" or even mention that fateful three-word sentence—I *love you*. The young girl may not understand why her chosen male counterpart does not reciprocate the same emotions. She may see him as being aloof, immature, or simply motivated by a physical drive, without any emotional attachment on his part. From the ambitious drive of men wanting to engage in sex to women not being emotionally understood by their male counterparts, the typical woman learns to *cope* with these distinct gender differences. For most women, this represents a catch-22. Men certainly seek their company, but the intention is clear as to what motivates the men to seek their company more often than not. There is yet another problem that needs to be discussed in this complex process—creating life.

A woman will invest a minimum of nine months of her life in resources, time, finances, and something she values highly—her emotional richness in create a new being in her body. On the other hand, a male can minimally invest a meager few minutes in creating a child during the act of sex. The woman has much more at risk in order to engage in and develop a relationship with her male partner. Still, experienced women are clear what they are risking when they first tell their prospective male partner—yes. It is clear that women have more at risk when the two sexes must unite in order to discover pleasure, enjoy life, create children, and grow together in a harmonious, beautiful, and powerful relationship.

In addition to difficulties previously mentioned, a woman must also deal with other problems, including the potential for men to be unfaithful or to be physically abused. It is easy to see how women can develop a cautionary approach in dealing with men in general. For the sake of fairness, most men also possess many great attributes. So there are women who are, through many painful experiences and having been in poor relationships with men, tend to develop poor strategies in dealing with men. These women will have nothing good to say about men. They do not trust men. These women do not want to engage with men, or they only use men for personal gain and may even intentionally inflict pain on them, in the form of sudden break-ups or toying with their partners emotions. Such is the extent that a woman who has been so immeasurably scarred is willing to go to in order to go on living.

So here lies a clear problem. Each gender can develop an unhealthy perspective about the opposite sex due to the potentially negative influences and experiences with the other gender. Each male and female who is *locked into* an unhealthy form of engaging the opposite sex has committed themselves to having more elements of anger, mistrust, and general disdain in their lives. So should we leave this poorly developed attitude alone? Perhaps, we can find certain elements of this sexist perspective within our own thoughts and developed concepts by identifying this sexist perspective. Being aware of your own pre-formed ideas, motives, and behaviors with the opposite sex is something that all people should take time to understand. Let us keep in mind that something can be done if a person wishes change in their life. A great starting point would be for people to be cognizant that they possess these developed perspectives. So what can be done?

A powerful understanding of discovering a new way of dealing with this issue is one based on developing great insights into human behavior. As mentioned earlier, we are the product of the many social and biological influences. We can, by reflection, see what factors have greatly contributed to our own ideas of becoming a man or a woman. If this is true, how is it that we cannot see how another person has also been sculpted into becoming the person they have become by their own set of influences and experiences? In order to heal ourselves from the many battle scars that go with dealing with engaging the opposite sex, we must be willing to understand what factors have shaped the other gender. We must find within ourselves the strength, courage, and forgiveness to deal with the opposite sex from this insightful perspective. We must afford ourselves the opportunity to heal. We must provide ourselves with the willingness to forgive and be respectful for the other gender's unique set of characteristics. After all, through the many relationships that we have encountered and been a part of, we have grown and matured. We have all gained from the ability to engage the opposite sex and become familiar with their differences, weaknesses, and strengths. So to assume a negative perspective with the opposite sex would only lead us to fewer opportunities to grow and be happy, and learn from the richness of the world around us. Let us not allow our mistrust and painful pre-conceptions about the opposite sex to misguide us or lead us astray. Let's not allow these negative emotions and ideas limit us. Instead let us be aware of these biased elements residing within us. Let us make a decision to do something different for ourselves, our loved ones, and those whom will continue to provide for us opportunities to continue to grow as a person and experience an enhanced qualitative life—the opposite sex.

If you have been single for a while and you are willing to engage the opposite sex, you will create for yourself more opportunities to nurture a relationship. If you are with the partner of your choice, you have already succeeded in overcoming many of these potential problems, inhibitions, cautious behaviors, or other predispositions that could have prevented you into developing the relationship you are in now.

Of the many approaches you can take to begin a new cycle in your life, one of the most outstanding approaches is to seek out counseling. Sure you can talk to your best friend(s) who may offer great advice, but they are not trained professionals in the field of psychology, counseling, nor do they have many years of practice as a therapist. Trained counselors benefit from years of studying human behavior, the human mind, human relationships, and how to help a person heal and retrain oneself into fostering new behaviors. It takes much effort and courage on your behalf to even consider wanting to go to these well-trained individuals. But it is one of the best opportunities you may have to help yourself heal and become whole once again.

A second option to approaching the idea of starting over is to simply begin shed your undesirable preconceptions. Slowly entertain the idea of starting fresh with someone new. In order to begin this process, you must give yourself opportunities in meeting new people. However, being sensitive in dealing with the opposite sex, it may be a good idea to have minimal contact with the opposite sex when first starting out. This is equivalent to immersing yourself into the water when wanting to visit the beach. You see the vastness of the sea before you, which represents the sea of potential partners you can choose to engage. Having almost drowned once (being in previously poor or non-nurturing relationships), you must afford yourself the opportunity to re-engage the opposite sex. You must first pick an area of the beach, which in itself represents a certain area of the community you want to find your potential partner. From there you must approach the water slowly once again, unless the memories and emotions of past poor relationships overwhelm you and you find yourself fleeing the beach altogether. For most people, it's a good idea to slowly put your toes in the water first. This represents having an open mind and heart, which are necessary for reconnecting with the opposite sex once again. Not in a spiteful way, but rather, in a wholesome approach that can be resurfaced from within you once again. You must search for which area of the incoming waves is the right temperature and feels comfortable for you. This represents the qualities that a person possesses, thus matching you suitability. You must then go ankle-deep into the water, which represents taking the next step in spending more time with that person to get to know them better. Once you have found the right thoughts and feelings within you, you will want to go knee-deep and enjoy the soothing comforts of the waves. This represents the richness of spending time with that person of your choice. Then you will find yourself waist-deep, which represents being exclusive with that person, having spent much time together already and knowing that person well enough to know that that is where you want to be. Lastly, you will find the waters up to your chest. This represents the idea that you have found the person whom you have chosen to be with as your new champion, just as they have chosen you to be their new champion. Once there, it is already too late and it would have been about time for this as well! Congratulations! You found within yourself the courage, drive, and ability to forgive. You have developed the opportunity to become whole through your new relationship.

The human condition of developing one's own gender identity is filled with many complex variables. It is within one's ability to experience the influences around oneself and make choices of how to respond to those influences. It is from these experiences that we develop and embrace our sexual identities. Being born either male or female is a tremendous opportunity that nature has granted us. From this opportunity to develop our sexual identity, we are afforded a method to express a part of the powerful movement of the human condition—to express our needs and desires through our self-developed concept of what it is to be a man or a woman.

The Biological Drive

From the early age of a male's teens, his human masculinity is driven by the commanding force of the biological drive; to engage in sexual activity. The male mind is consistently bombarded by thoughts of sexual encounters with a female. The woman from the early onset of menarche during her teens is signaled that her body is ready to create life. However, her need to engage in sexual encounters is different from that of a male's. Society, culture, and even a strict family upbringing will tell her that she cannot pursue her sexual urges as a male is freely allowed to do. The woman is strongly influenced by her environment to demonstrate etiquette and properness. Nonetheless, a woman also has a strong biological drive to reproduce which can be seen commonly in her early to mid-twenties. The financial, mental, emotional, and social costs to a couple of having a child are great. Still, couples are driven toward this powerful biological and social process. In order to best understand the sexual drives that dictate much of our behaviors, we need to briefly discuss the biological process that induces the physiological events occurring in the body of both sexes. Let us discuss the creation of hormones and their functions in the human body, and how these hormones vastly affect how as a person we come to be.

There are two main sex hormones many people are familiar with—testosterone and estrogen. Some of the effects that have been attributed to testosterone have been aggressive male behavior. Estrogen has been associated with a woman expressing strong emotional instincts. The need to understand how these powerful hormones affect the human body are an important part of understanding one of the building blocks of human relationships—engaging in sexual activity. Testosterone and estrogen are made in the body from a fat molecule commonly found in the diet—cholesterol, which in itself, is a building block for this same hormone.

Cholesterol is one of the three main sources of fat consumed in the diet. The body has the ability to transform cholesterol into a hormone through various biochemical processes (biochemical processes are the body's cells producing chemicals in order to achieve a balance state in the cell and the body). Testosterone is created from cholesterol in the leydig cells (specialized cells found exclusively in male testicles). In these leydig cells of the testes, cholesterol is changed into various chemical structures until it reaches its biochemical goal—the production of testosterone. The created testosterone can then locally support the production of sperm in the testes (this process is term spermatogenesis). Testosterone also circulates from the testicles to other sites of the body which supports the production of secondary sexual characteristics (more upper body muscles mass, deeper voice, facial hair, etc.), which are the trademarks for the male body and an aggressive nature to the male so as to afford himself more opportunities to mate. Regulation of the production of testosterone in the body actually occurs in the brain. The brain, for some as yet not fully understood reason, informs a powerful regulatory area within itself called the hypothalamus (master hormone regulatory center) to release Gonadotropin-releasing hormone (GRH). This GRH then goes from the hypothalamus to the anterior pituitary gland (attached to the hypothalamus) to stimulate the release of a two hormones called follicle-stimulating hormone (FSH) and luteinizing hormone (LH).

LH stimulates the testicle's leydig cells to produce more testosterone in support of spermatogenesis, along with the required secondary sexual characteristics. FSH supports spermatogenesis, although not to the degree that LH does in the male's body. Since the brain can, at will, support the development of testosterone at a desirable level, this adjusting ability in the brain to either rev up or tone down its level of testosterone production indicates a capacity within the male body to create the amount of testosterone it needs (there being both a peak limit and a minimal limit to the amount of testosterone that the body can generate). The brain thus creates the desired testosterone levels in order to accomplish a goal—to promote a healthy pursuit of and engagement in sexual activity. An example of the male's body to generate the amount of testosterone it deems necessary can be seen in males who are involved in long-term relationships, such as being married and raising a family. In this situation, the male has already succeeded in finding himself a mate. In these men, testosterone levels in the blood are known to be lower than in males who are single and are not in a long-term relationship. Single males will typically require higher dosages of testosterone coursing through their bodies in order to become more competitive with the other males who are also seeking a female partner. The increased levels of testosterone can also enhance the secondary sexual male characteristics along with the required aggressive male behavior to be more successful in this endeavor.

So the male body, regulated by the male brain, can *rev up* or *rev down* its production of testosterone according to its environmental needs. Men also produce estrogen in small quantities, which is the further conversion of testosterone to estradiol within the leydig cells, albeit in small quantities. It is well known that the tiny amount of estrogen in the male body that is produced stays constant as the male goes into his menopausal state (due to his decreasing levels of testosterone being produced by the testes) as a male goes into his mid-forties and beyond. This shifting of the dominant hormone of testosterone to estrogen in the male body begins to affect the older male's body with a consequential loss of the male's distinguishable secondary sexual characteristics. Along with this gradual loss of physical male attractiveness comes a decreased mental drive to emphasize the need for constant sexual engagements. Interestingly enough, the male, for the second time in his life (the first time was before puberty), begins to emphasize other mental focuses in his life with more clarity. This clarity can be seen in males reaching their late forties and early fifties who are known to reach their intellectual peaks during this time. Here the male is better positioned to develop other areas of interests with his mental activities than the constantly demanding sexual drive urges he would previously contend with. The development of hormones and their effects in a female body has a more complex explanation to it.

The woman has been given the responsibility of propagating the human species by a two-fold ability—to create life in her body and provide the newborn with its essential physical, emotional, and mental needs. Such a complex reproductive and nurturing ability requires a more physiologically complex human body to be able to fulfill such a demanding role. This complexity is reflected in a woman's regulatory hormonal activity. Unlike a male, whose body is dominated by testosterone, a woman's body is by a few cyclically controlled reproductive hormones. These hormones are estrogen, progesterone, and testosterone. Let us first discuss estrogen.

The hormone estrogen (estradiol) is the primary hormone. This provides the woman with her secondary sexual characteristics, as mentioned earlier. Estrogen is produced primarily in her two ovaries. As with testosterone, estrogen is generated from the fat molecule cholesterol which is obtained from the diet. Cholesterol is converted to testosterone, which is further converted to estradiol in specialized cells in the ovaries called the granulosa cells. Estrogen actually comes in three forms: estrone, estriol, and estradiol. Estrodiol is the predominant hormone that the female body used for promoting her secondary sexual characteristics during her reproductive years, such as having developed breasts, the redistribution of fat in her body to emphasize a smaller hip-to-waist ratio, and a high-pitched voice implying high levels of estrogen in her body. The estrogen also maintains her reproductive abilities, such as maintaining the vaginal lining optimal for sexual activity, keeping the myometrium in the uterus (the lining of the uterus where the fertilized egg can attach itself to) in a healthy state, and maintaining an optimal lining in her fallopian tubes to assist the egg down its long journey. The high level of estrogen also promotes a woman's female prowess by having her behave in such a way as to advertise her sexual reproductive capacity, as can be seen when a woman will walk to emphasize the movement of her bottom, which in turn promotes her chances of attracting a mate. Another example of this type of activity would be when she becomes more flirtatious with men.

There are two other forms of estrogen. Estriol is the form of estrogen used when the woman is pregnant. Estrone is a less potent form of estradiol and is produced after the onset of menopause. Thus, depending upon a woman's reproductive condition, she too can alternate the type of estrogen her body requires in order to accomplish her powerfully biological needs.

Progesterone is the second hormone dominant in a woman's body. Progesterone and estrogen coordinate the development and growth of the follicle (eggs) of the ovaries. They also promote the endometrial lining of the uterus to prepare the uterus for a successful implantation of an egg that has been fertilized. The balancing of estrogen and progesterone's activity in a woman's body flow in a cyclical balance can be referred to as a woman's menstrual cycle. The menstrual cycle lasts approximately 28 days (which is believed to be coordinated with the lunar cycle). During this 28-day time period, her body provides her with the opportunity to become impregnated, and if unsuccessful, regenerate or activate specific anatomical tissue (such as the endometrial lining of the uterus being regenerated and the ovary's eggs being activated) so as to begin the process anew. As mentioned previously, the hormones FSH and LH regulate estrogen and progesterone levels. As a new menstrual cycle begins, a large amount of FSH is released from the anterior pituitary. This sudden elevated level of released FSH reaches the granulosa cells in the ovaries, which promotes an increase in estrogen production in these cells. This increased estrogen production stimulates the simultaneous recruitment and development of several follicles in the ovary (the ovary which had not been used in the previous menstrual cycle).

In a period of fourteen days the eggs most developed out of the batch of recruited eggs which can number approximately between 5 to 19, all compete with each other and only the dominant egg and wins the opportunity to become fertilized, thus releasing itself from the physical confines of the ovary through the process termed ovulation. It then begins its great journey through the reproductive tract of the body (down the fallopian tubes and into the uterine lining). It also creates a higher than normal amount of estrogen, which signals the hypothalamus that the egg has successfully developed. This hormonal message then signals the hypothalamus to release a large amount of LH from the pituitary gland. This sudden release of LH signals the endometrial lining of the uterus to prepare itself for possible implantation by a fertilized egg. This is known as proliferation of the uterus lining. This phase of the menstrual cycle is called the luteal phase, and it lasts approximately fourteen days. If such an egg becomes fertilized within the reproductive tract within the five- to seven-day window, the fertilized egg implants itself onto the endometrial lining of the uterus where it begins to create another powerful hormone called gonadotropin-releasing hormone (GRH). This hormone signals the body that fertilization was successful and implantation was complete—a zygote is born (a fertilized cell that will begin to divide and develop into a healthy newborn nine months later).

The menstrual cycle begins with the follicular phase (where menstruation caused by the previous cycle begins) and ends with the luteal phase (where no implantation occurred), only to start anew. Interestingly enough, just when the estrogen level drops (after the follicle has been released from the ovary), the constant level of testosterone in the female's body has the effect of promoting the woman's behavior to seek out a male partner so as to promote impregnation. The single woman will create more opportunities to socialize by calling up male contacts or simply seeking out male company at home, work, or in other areas of the community. The woman with her chosen partner will be more accepting and will initiate sexual activity. Another example of this type of sexually driven behavior is when a woman is willing to change her attire, so as to show off more of her secondary sexual characteristics such as her hips, bottom, or cleavage, along with more of her skin on her shoulders or legs. This is a very natural and healthy sexually driven behavior for a woman during this phase of her reproductive cycle.

I have briefly discussed some of the fundamental sexual physiological processes of both sexes. A medical book or a website can be accessed to clarify any additional questions if you are curious of such as how the complex process of a woman's body ability to create life progresses or how a man's body works. There is, however, an influence that the hormones estrogen and testosterone have on the brain.

It is well known that the human male and female brain each have innate skills/tasks that the other sex usually does not express. According to Jensen (2008), the male and female brains have a stronger ability to accomplish the following feats:

Male brain:
- Targeting skills
- Working vocabulary
- Extended focus and concentration
- Mathematical reasoning and problem solving aptitude
- Navigation with geometric properties of space
- Verbal intelligence
- Habit formation and maintenance
- Most spatial tasks

Female brain:
- Fine motor skills
- Computation tests
- Multitasking
- Recalling the position of objects in an array
- Spelling
- Fluency of word generation
- Tasks that require being sensitive to external stimuli (except visual stimuli)
- Remembering landmarks along a route
- Verbal recall
- Appreciation of depth and perceptual speed
- Reading body language and facial expressions[9]

---

[9] Jensen, E. (2008). *Brain Based Learning (2nd Edition)*. Corwin Press. Thousand Oaks, CA.

It is not clear to what extent testosterone affects the male brain to predispose it to such feats or to what extent estrogen influences the female brain to develop such skills/abilities. Further neuroscience investigation is required to show why this is the case. For now, it is clear that these tendencies in the brain are common gender traits. With this said however, it is important to accept the idea that we seem to be hard-wired to be who we are, in part because of which hormone flows in greater amount through our bodies. This fact is not to be taken as a harsh lesson in accepting the opposite sex's way of being. Rather, it can be used as a stepping stone for reaching out to gain a better understanding of the opposite sex.

Let us be open-minded about the other sex's perspective of their reproductive drive. As a male, it is difficult to understand the complexity of a woman's body and her behavioral patterns to express herself through her emotions. Men often see women as being aloof and indirect about some of their intentions. Men would prefer that women were simply direct with their thoughts and behaviors. In particular, when it comes to the act of sexual activity, men would prefer that women would want to engage in sex more often, just as they are inclined to do. Well, gentlemen, keep in mind that the hormone testosterone is the main drive for your constant sexual drive. Testosterone runs approximately more than ten times higher in your body than it does in a woman's body. This is one reason why women do not have such a strong sexual drive in general. Along these lines, women are more at risk of becoming pregnant, after which she will endure nine months of incredible changes to her body in order to successfully create life and assist propagating the human species. We gentlemen will, at a minimum, donate three minutes. A woman will risk pregnancy, potential physical abuse, exposure to sexually transmitted diseases, and her invested emotional essence damaged (something a woman holds very dearly), along with a host of other risks. Understanding what a woman is sacrificing when she is offering her physical body to you gentlemen is absolutely essential for you to understand. She does not offer her physical body alone (that is if this is not

50

a brief overnight sexual encounter), she will also be offering her heart, her mind, and basically the essence of her being in general. This is a sacrifice that a male can never fully capture. And yet, she, knowing that you do not fully understand her, is still willing to offer all of these gifts to you, her chosen companion, in the name of building a relationship. Such an amazing perspective *must* be captivated by us, gentlemen. This is the tremendous gift a woman offers you when she is willing to share intimate moments with you.

For the women, yes, it appears that the men are driven by a strong sexual drive. Yes, men seem so superficial at times to your perspective. But keep in mind that men have high levels of testosterone coursing through their blood. It is a constant, powerful, biological drive. Ladies, if you can recall when you get the urge to engage in sexual activity when your body is primed to become pregnant (due to the lower than normal estrogen levels which makes your body pay attention to the constant low level of testosterone), the testosterone that is strongly driving you toward engaging in sexual activity is actually three times lower than what a male usually has at his lowest physiological level. Keep in mind that if a woman were to assume the same attitude as men—let them control their sexual drives, then it would be fair for the men to ask of the women in return—please control your regulatory cycle of wanting to reproduce as well! Of course, this task is challenging for men and impossible for women (unless you, as a lady, are already using hormone contraceptives; but even this approach to controlling your body's reproductive ability does not stop your bodies from constantly producing estrogen and progesterone, just as the male is unable to control his high levels of testosterone production, which pushes him toward his constant sexual drive). Ladies, keep in mind that the male is biologically compelled to reproduce constantly. It is one of his main physiological functions to do so. You ladies are also compelled to reproduce, be it in cyclical patterns, but nonetheless the biological drive is also a powerfully compelling force within you. If we keep this perspective in mind for the opposite sex, perhaps we can find understanding, tolerance, acceptance, and even benefits of the other sex's patterns of biological behavior. Thus, we gain deep insights into who our companion is.

Would not the best approach to tolerating the other sex's behavior best be served by understanding the other sex and developing a tolerance for their behavior? Seeing that we, as a species, are committed to our respective inherited sexual identity, can we not come to understand that we must learn to live together, work together, and even love together? It is through engagements, developing relationships, and committing with that special chosen partner that we can develop a prosperous and joyful life. Such an approach to dealing with the opposite sex can bring about the best of potential outcomes between the two sexes. A cooperative spirit of working with the opposite sex is fundamental to tolerating, and ultimately, flourishing together.

The need for the human species to proliferate is a powerfully biological drive that the human mind is only occasionally conscious of. Many of the behaviors we exhibit daily are motivated by this most influential basic instinct. As stated earlier, from entering into new relationships to committing to long-term relationships, these actions provide us with the life-granting opportunity to perpetuate the species as well as provide for our progeny the foundation for a successful upbringing. There are other motivational factors involved in the act of sex. It can provide an outlet of grasping pleasurable sensations and expressing the outflow of emotional countenance from within the recesses of the heart. It can create an opportunity to become vulnerable to our chosen partners, a form of dominating and being dominated by our partners, and generally bonding to the one we love as we learn to give and to receive with our partner. The act of sex is a true dynamic, powerful, and intense human experience. Sex is an outlet of human expression which stems from several fundamental human needs. Through this very natural and powerful human experience we are afforded the opportunity to create a new life and engage in other forms of self-expression. Not a bad deal for both genders.

The Four Levels of Human Development--Their Attributes

In this chapter we will explore how to find a compatible companion based on personal growth along four areas of human development. These four areas of human development are: physical, emotional, mental, and spiritual. Through the development of these attributes, we advertise ourselves to our perspective partners.

As we journey through life, we connect with many people along the way. Being the social creatures that we are, we tend to find companions, friends, colleagues, or groups of people we tend to related and thus are drawn to. As we connect with others, we tend to assess another person's personal growth levels in terms of how they have developed. Often, we will compare ourselves to them (which is a natural human tendency). As we compare ourselves to others, we will have one of three possible reactions: a dis-taste, indifference, or admiration for another person's attributes. If we come to have a dis-taste for a particular characteristic of their personality, we may tend to stay away from them or simply not like them. If we react indifferently to an aspect of their character or personal growth, we may or may not use this fact to assess them or simply ignore this attribute about them. However, if we admire an area of their personal growth, we may find ourselves respecting them and being drawn to them. In some cases, we will find these individuals to be appealing to us, especially if they are of the opposite sex we will find them attractive. For we will, through our own desire to grow, want to somehow acquire from them or have these individuals tutor us in these desirable aspects to themselves. Let us discuss in some detail these four areas of personal growth which can further understand our own motivations of why we are often attracted to the opposite sex. Let us begin with the physical attributes of people.

Physical attributes advertise what a person has genetically available for biological, reproductive purposes. It is through these physical attributes that people demonstrate what we find attractive. A person advertises many physical attributes. Everyone is attracted to a person who has healthy skin, a healthy body, and attractive physical features. People also assess other people's attractiveness based on preferred physical features, such as a potential partner having a particular hair or eye color, skin tone, the symmetry of one's face and other personal traits that one would find subconsciously driven by prior positive experiences a person may have had with other people. There seem to be, however, physical traits for both men and women that the opposite sex finds to be universally attractive.

A more abstract but consistently mathematical finding observed throughout nature and found within the concept of human beauty is called the Phi ratio (the golden ratio). This Phi ratio is a distinct ratio of 1 to 1.1618 and it can found in many objects in nature that we find appealing to our eyes such as flowers having a dispersal pattern of petals to the stamen. This ratio can also be found in animals, buildings, people's faces, etc. In the search for an explanation of what beauty is, this ratio can be found on the human face and body as well. The more that this ratio can be found on a human face and body, the more that person will be found attractive in general. There are also universal features found in both sexes that are known to be trademarks of physical attractiveness. Let us first discuss this universal concept of beauty in bodily features that women can possess that makes them physically attractive to the opposite sex.

Female attractiveness is often tied to the ability to reproduce, which in turn is tied to universal concepts of female beauty. Extensive research supports this position. According to Brooks (2010), where 96 bodies of students and volunteers from Hong Kong were studied by Hong Kong and Australian men and women, his team found the following: women who were younger (youthfulness), taller, and lighter in skin tone were considered more attractive. Also, women with a narrower waistline relative to their height, also were considered more attractive. In general, people falling within the norm of the Body/Mass-Index (BMI) – which is the weight of the person relative to their height and who had a hip-to-waist ratio (HWR) of 0.7 were more likely considered to be attractive.[10] An article by Siegfried (2012), states that the appearance of good physical health seems to be a universally attractive feature of women.[11] This is also true for men. The article also briefly discussed other features that women can possess that would be considered universally attractive in general. These features included:

- unblemished skin
- lustrous and vibrant long hair (due to the biological idea that only healthy women can grow long hair)
- having fuller hips and buttocks (0.7 ratio to demonstrate childbearing capacity)
- the ability to demonstrate the whiteness of your teeth (the whiter the teeth the more healthier) by the act of smiling more often
- sitting or standing with an erect posture (demonstrating energy and vigilance for seeking out a potential mating partner)
- women demonstrating a natural vibrant energy level in their activities
- demonstrating good personal cleanliness and hygiene

These traits are considered universally attractive female traits. Of course, a large set of eyes and thinly raised eyebrows to accentuate the size of the eyes which creates a cuteness (vulnerability) and full lips (to demonstrate subconsciously the fullness of the woman's labia) are also attractive features of a

---

[10] 1.R. Brooks, J. P. Shelly, J. Fan, L. Zhai, D. K. P. Chau. Much more than a ratio: multivariate selection on female bodies. Journal of Evolutionary Biology, 2010; 23 (10): 2238

[11] Siegfried, J. (2012). Physical Traits That Are Universally Attractive in Both Men and Women. Health Guidance: Health Guidance for better health. Retrieved from: http://www.healthguidance.org/entry/16417/1/Physical-Traits-That-Are-Universally-Attractive-in-Men-and-Women.html

woman. Another feature that can contrast a woman's body from a man's would be her breasts. A woman possessing a generous set of breasts (which also indicates the ability to nurture the newborn), is endowed with a strong physical reproductive trait which in turn demonstrates a universal physical attractive feature.

Let us now discuss what universal physical features a man may possess that women would find attractive. Continuing on with Siegfried's article, there are many universal features that men can possess that women can find physically attractive. These include:

- healthy looking body
- unblemished skin
- lustrous and vibrant hair
- Classic "V" shaped torso (demonstrating upper body strength)
- Strong shoulders and arms (demonstrating an ability to protect)
- Waist-to-hip ratio of 1.0
- the ability to demonstrate the whiteness of your teeth by smiling more often
- sitting or standing with an erect posture
- demonstrating a natural vibrant energy level in one's activities
- demonstrate good personal cleanliness and personal hygiene

An article written by Houran (2010), also speaks of universal attractive features of men which also includes the following:

- Men with substantial height (to demonstrate aspects of good protectors)
- Wide brow and a square jaw (dominating features of ruggedness)

- Average features of a face and body (not excessive physical features to demonstrate an absence of genetic defects)[12]

These are some of the major physical attributes that are allotted to men in general.

In the end, it is the ability of women to demonstrate their level of estrogen which demonstrates her reproductive abilities and her ability to nurture a child. For the man, it is his ability to demonstrate health so as to successfully inseminate the woman as well as his ability to protect. Our biological drive is so ingrained within us, that our social structure, culture, and even our family exposure will have driven into our minds these essential concepts to be considered physically attractive. It is also a genetically inherited drive that dictates what conveys to us how capable a person is of reproducing. For example, in aboriginal societies one can often find these relevant universal features ingrained into their societies. This indicates that our brains are genetically programmed to these patterns of thoughts and behaviors that dictate what we find physically attractive.

However, what we find attractive is not solely based on these concepts. We often have preconceptions based on previous experiences from having engaged other people in our past. For example, if a young girl has a vague recollection of a bald gentleman being kind to her during a time of need, she will likely associate bald gentlemen with inner beauty. As a woman, she may likely find bald men attractive. Another possibility would be as a young boy who remembers a lovely and caring elementary teacher that he had a crush on always wearing prescription glasses and being professionally dressed. Later, as a man, he may inexplicably find women dressed professionally and wearing prescription glasses to be attractive. On the contrary, you may recall as a young girl a

---

[12] Houran, J. (2010). Universal Attraction and Physical attributes. Online Dating Magazine. Retrieved from:
http://www.onlinedatingmagazine.com/columns/drjim/2007/12-universallyattractive.html#1

man who wore his hair parted down the middle who may have made you uncomfortable or was cruel. Later, you may find yourself not want to deal with men with hair parted down the middle. There are many more examples of why one may find certain features people demonstrate as being attractive or unattractive. These given examples are psychological predispositions that reside in your subconscious mind which can explain why you find a person attractive and you have no clue why.

When all is said and done, the physical attributes that a person demonstrates are always being noticed by the people around them. The reasons why people may find themselves physically attracted to someone else – whether they're based on biology or psychological predispositions – are complex and various. These are by no means the only reason why this is so. There are many other reasons for attraction to the opposite sex, such as people possessing wealth, positions of influence over other people, and people who are well known in certain circles for their accomplishments. However, people in general are noticed by other people. As the people noticing, we are attracted to the physical characteristics of other people by their physical attributes, which appeal to our inner compass of what we define physical sexual appeal to be.

To this point, we have been referring exclusively to the exterior aspect of a person. There are many forms by which a person can be considered to be beautiful beyond exterior beauty. The other qualities to be further considered can be referred to as the inner attributes of a person's beauty. Many other areas which can be considered as being attributes of inner beauty may include savvy, intelligence, suave, charm, confidence, elegance, musical expertise, charisma, and even a strong drive toward spiritual values, to name a few. These areas can be developed by the other three potential areas of human growth, which include emotional, mental, and spiritual traits. Let us discuss the next level of development a person could refine and mature, so as to attribute to that person's attractiveness — emotional development. Let us discuss what emotions are and explain how they play a role in assessing, through our emotional needs, what we find attractive in others.

Emotional experience is a powerful contribution to the human condition. Imagine what life would be like without being able to experience emotions? This scenario is not possible, because just the thought of experiencing life without emotions, immediately conjures up emotional responses. As discussed in a chapter in my book, MY DEEP Training: An Uncommon Guide Toward Spiritual Growth and General Well Being, emotions assist the mind in prioritizing the relevance of experiences in daily life. This ability of the mind to prioritize experiences either from the past or the present helps us learn from the experiences we have today and even offer some predictability to anticipated future events. Emotions also can offer the human mind the ability to acquire from our experiences more than just the experiences themselves. Emotions allow us to experience our lives more passionately, which provides more powerful and insightful conclusions about experiences. This in turn will serve us to survive and adapt better in our given environments. Emotions are another tool evolution has provided us to better survive.

Neuroscientists tell us that emotions stem from a part of the brain called the limbic system. The limbic system is located deep within the tissue of the brain and can be further sub-divided into certain anatomical areas within the brain. The hippocampus and the amygdale are two sub-divided areas within the limbic system that are known to specifically provide for the brain the ability to provide memory and process emotional content respectively. The hippocampus is the anatomical site known to store memory for the brain. Next to the hippocampus is the amygdala. Here, incoming information from the senses, recollection information about the past (through the hippocampus), or current information being processed through the brain is processed through the amygdala, where what I would term *tagging,* of this incoming information occurs. *Tagging* refers to associating an emotional response to this incoming information that is being processed. For example, imagine taking a casual walk when you happen to see a beautiful colored bird in the trees. To your delight, you notice the bird chirping some unfamiliar sound. Being that you are a lover of the outdoors, you associate this experience as pleasant. In later events, you'll be likely to associate similar experiences to that previous experience as being pleasant. Another example would be mentioning the name of your parents. Depending on the type of experience you've had with your parents, you will associate either positive emotions or negative emotions. But an emotional reaction will most like follow with just the mention of your parents. This is the concept of emotional processing. Emotions themselves can be further classified.

Emotions can be basically classified as negative or positive. Strong negative emotions such as anger, fear, or hate are well known. Positive emotions such as love, joy, and jubilation are highly sought-out emotions. Since the human brain has been developed through evolution, it has the ability to experience these emotions. As an excerpt, animals such as reptiles, birds, amphibians, and mammals all possess a brain structure with similar but smaller structures than the human brain. This anatomically available brain feature in turn must provide for them primitive emotions, such as fear and anger as well as some other forms of positively constructed emotions. It is believed among the neuroscience community that the more complex the brain structure, the more complex the ability to generate complex outcomes. Among these outcomes are complex emotional expressions such as love, compassion or empathy. Thus, both positive and negative emotions are essential to survival.

People are born with the ability to experience emotions. If you can recall seeing your child being born, or if you have ever walked into a newborn nursery in a hospital where the infants can be in either in emotional distress (crying) or in a state of ease (sleeping), this can easily confirm that even newborns have emotional abilities at birth. The amygdala is sufficiently developed at birth to cope with stressful and serene moments. The hippocampus is developed (allowing memory to form), but it is not at its functional peak until the age of two or three where long term memories begin to be established. As we pass through the initial bonding stages with our mothers, we learn to comprehend deeper emotions such as attachment, joy, and even expressions of laughter as one can easily recall if they have spent a sufficient amount of time tending to their newborns and toddlers. As new experiences are novelties to toddlers, the world seems rich in learning great and wonderful things. In this way, emotions are used to capture the relevance of these experiences and to assist our ability to configure their relevance to new experiences. So humans continue to expand their repertoire of experiences, and through these experiences, they expand their abilities to adapt to their environmental states. As a person matures, so does their emotional capacity. This is demonstrated by thoughts and behaviors. However, men and women develop their emotional abilities differently.

It is well known that most females express more emotions than males. The brains of females tend to develop stronger emotional capacity than men do. It is believed that estradiol has some degree of influence on the genetic female brain, even while the brain is developing *in utero* (in the womb of the mother). A possible result of the influence of the estradiol hormone on the female brain is a somewhat larger developed amygdala area, where emotions are processed. Since the female brain has a larger amygdala, she then must also have a larger capacity to experience emotions than her male counterpart. Females of all ages experience life with a heightened cognitive ability. Let us call this ability a *heightened cognitive-sense*. This heightened cognitive-sense endows females with the ability to experience life with more emotional intensity, at a depth that very few men who are able to reach (unless a man is born with a similarly sized and capable amygdala). Therefore, from this evolutionary capacity, a woman experiences life differently than a man does. This heightened ability has been given to women, in part, due to the need to nurture their offspring from the in-utero phase to the well-developed adult phase and beyond. I am confident that another reason why women have a stronger ability to express emotions would be to not only develop a bond that maintains a family structure but also creates a gender-appealing quality.

Females possess a gender specific quality that appeals to the male. This quality affords us men with the capacity to become vulnerable to another human being. Through that vulnerability comes an increased bonding between couples. This ability cannot be easily afforded between males. In the presence of a female, a male can be given tacit permission to get in touch with his emotions. While reacquainting himself with his emotions, he will feel vulnerable to himself and to his female companion. He can be encouraged to continue being in touch with his emotions by his emotionally savvy partner and even reflect upon his ability to grow in this destitute capacity. Of course, not all men are so disadvantaged. Depending upon childhood circumstances, such as having a loving, nurturing mother, some men will have developed their emotional capacity and will grow to become healthy, emotionally functional, human males.

Of course, these well-developed emotional males still will not be able to fully understand the intensity and depth that the average woman experiences on a day-to-day basis. Keep in mind that women from childhood are encouraged to express their emotions in their family-structured upbringing, within their cultural boundaries, and by the society that nurtured them. Girls in childhood and adolescent girls are often holding hands, hugging each other, talking about their feelings, or often writing in their personal journals. Organized women in society form women's clubs, organizations, and associations that also encourage these types of strong expressions of communication. It is clear that women experience a different world than men. This difference brings us to a misunderstanding between the sexes in communicating, relating to one another, and of course, in forming long-term relationships. Still, with each gender having their own level of emotional development well-established, these attributes tend to be noticed and admired by the opposite sex. Here is where the emotional quotient comes into play.

As we engage in our lives, we have the ability to learn, grow, and adapt from the events and people we experience. Our emotional capacity grows along with our intellectual development. We develop our ability to love, be understanding, and tolerant of our own shortcomings and those of others. As we develop these skills, we mature into our own ability to evolve emotionally. The more emotionally evolved one is, the more they are able to accept themselves and accept others for the person they are. This level of developed emotional expressions one can obtain is an admirable characteristic that they can demonstrate to the world. This unique characteristic to be loving, gentle, patient, generous, and empathic is highly sought out and is a very attractive feature. Emotionally developed individuals resonate an aura of positive emotional characteristics. People who possess high emotional intelligence tend to be skillful at interpreting, understanding, and dealing with their own emotions and the emotions of others. These individuals are well suited for dealing with social or emotional conflicts. They are also capable of being open about their own feelings and dealing with emotional situations.

Women have more of an evolved emotional depth and capacity than men. This emotional capacity that women possess is a strong appealing component that attracts men. That said, some men also resonate their own distinct emotional maturity that is appealing to women as well. We often come across people who are well developed in this capacity in our daily lives. When we do come across these emotionally evolved individuals, we tend to gravitate toward them. We want to connect with them, learn from them, and be part of their lives. Although this quality to people is present, men and women have different focuses when choosing a partner, however.

When beginning a relationship with someone we find interesting, emotional maturity is, to be honest, not one of the attributes we first notice. We initially are drawn toward our chosen partner by their physical attributes. Generally speaking, men will tend to focus on the physical attributes of their female partners as the days and weeks pass. More mature men will ask their prospective partner of her background, her family, her profession, even about some of her past relationships. On the other hand, women tend to be more adept at investigating a man's profession, past relationships, family background, and their level of emotional maturity. They will be likely to do so more quickly. Since women generally demonstrate a need to quickly assess the attributes of their perspective males, due in part to their biological clocks ticking as well as assessing their compatibility with their perspective partners. One of a woman's essential needs is a male that is emotionally compatible, especially if the woman herself is into her mid-twenties and beyond. So what are some of these qualities that some people possess that draws us in as a moth is drawn to the light? What are some of these attributes of emotional maturity?

There are four factors that define the concept of emotional intelligence:

- The perception of emotions—to accurately perceive which emotions are being expressed.
- The ability to reason using emotions—to use emotions to promote thinking and cognitive ability, such as when to prioritize experiences when our emotions prioritize these experiences.
- The ability to understand emotions—attempting to understand the emotional response being expressed by oneself and others and how it came about.
- The ability to manage emotions—this is the highest aspect of emotional intelligence, in which a person has developed the ability to regulate emotions; responding well to other's emotions as well as to one's own internal emotional state.[13]

So what traits do these emotionally intelligent individuals possess? These individuals are skilled at: decision-making, time management, empathy, stress management, anger management skills, trust, assertiveness, accountability,

---

[13] Cherry, K. (2012). What Is Emotional Intelligence? About.Com. Psychology. Retrieved from:
http://psychology.about.com/od/personalitydevelopment/a/emotionalintell.htm

flexibility, strong social skills, and communication.[14] These individuals have developed their feelings so as to use them as a resource for interacting with the world. They are so familiar with their emotional capacity that they are in control of their emotions versus having their emotions controlling them. Having evolved to this point, these individuals are also able to better understand the emotional states of others. They can assist others with their own individual emotional needs and experiences. These individuals will also have learned how to skillfully minimize negative or undesirable emotions, such as anger, hate, or sadness. These individuals will often demonstrate a strong ability to make you comfortable with them. They will be generous with their emotions and demonstrate genuine empathy with you, especially with respect to conversations that involve sharing areas of concern in your life. This is why an emotionally mature individual is so appealing to people. This is a highly attractive attribute that people seek out in others. This is also why women, since their emotions are typically more mature than those of men, can be so appealing to men. Opportunities can become available here for both parties to grow with such differences between the sexes.

Women are highly skilled at being in touch with their emotions, often because they have acknowledged and worked with them so intensely from such a young age. Men are more often lacking in emotional capacity (due to their brain's amygdala not being as well developed and not being encouraged by society to work with their emotions). It's important for men to keep in mind that women are highly skilled in dealing and working with their emotions. This ability is given to them from birth, just as men were given the ability to have more upper body strength.. Women experience a world very different from men. Part of the reason is this heightened sense of emotional existence. Women dwell in this higher plane of emotional existence. Would it not be wiser for

---

[14] Schmidt, M. (2012). About Emotional Intelligence: What Everybody Needs to Know. Talent Smart. Retrieved from:
http://www.talentsmart.com/about/emotional-intelligence.php

us gentlemen, in order to better understand our female companions, attempt to see the world through their enhanced emotional capacity? This would demonstrate a strong gesture on our part to connect with them and love them. In order to better connect with our female companion, we must learn to get in touch with our own emotions gentlemen. While alone with our lady partner, we should feel comfortable enough and even encouraged by our partner to express to them our emotions. We should even learn to be comfortable enough to work and develop our emotional state while being guided by them. After all, they are usually experts in this area of human development. Our weaknesses as human males can turn into a strength with time and effort. In time we males can be a more suitable companion for that female champion we have chosen to live our lives with. In turn, our female companions will love us more deeply and admire us more for showing her courage and trust while being vulnerable before them. In addition, we will become a more suitable companion.

As for women, knowing that men possess a decreased capacity to express themselves emotionally and that you are required to exist in such a heightened state of existence – knowing that you are more skilled in this human capacity (as well as being such nurturing individuals) – why not encourage to have your male partners gently open themselves up to you emotionally? This could include providing for the both of you intimate settings and giving him time to share his thoughts and feelings about anything he wants to. This approach to male emotional expression will heed great rewards. Ladies, you want a partner that is emotionally expressive and willing to grow in this capacity—the perfect mate for you! With much effort and patience, you can achieve many rewards with your willing companion. Such are the opportunities that lie between a man and the woman.

Emotions are a powerful tool that nature has provided the human mind. Through emotions, our lives are greatly enriched and amplified. Men and women possess different states of emotional capacity. Both forms of emotional maturity often make a person more appealing to the opposite sex. This can draw us toward our potential partner. Although physical attraction is the first step in being drawn to another person's company, emotional attraction becomes one of the preferred factors in relationships in the long run. This, in turn, promotes longer relationships. Although not apparent to the naked eye, emotional appeal becomes a powerful capacity to appreciate and pursue in another. There is, however, another component to the human potential that can draw us in—human intellect.

Human intelligence is an admirable quality. We humans are capable of creating almost anything we can conceive. Humans seemingly possess a greater intelligence among the animal world. This can be attributed to the evolutionary growth of the human brain over millions of years of development. Known to possess a weight of approximately 3-5 pounds, the human brain consists of neurons, which number to hundreds of billions of cells. The brain also consists of white matter cells. These white matter cells contribute to the connecting of one gray matter neuron to potentially thousands of other neurons. This fact demonstrates the importance of white matter cells in the human brain. With both types of brain cells combined, effective cooperation between these cell types (as well as proposed hundreds of other cell types which also contribute towards the functioning of the brain) creates the ability for the brain to make more connections within itself than there are proposed stars in our known universe! Even more startling is the fact that the human brain is constantly re-wiring itself to accommodate for the endless need for a human being to adapt to the ever-growing environmental changes.

In other words, the human brain is constantly learning. It adapts its own physical structure as it grows. As diverse as people are, so are the capable attributes which the human brain can generate. These attributes are well-demonstrated, as people are engaged in their daily activities and when they interact with other people. Often we can be taken away by another person's mental attributes, which in itself becomes an attractive feature to that individual.

We have all been mesmerized by the demonstration of another person's mental abilities. Who has not sat in a classroom where we were so impressed by a classmate demonstrating their knowledge, insights, or just showing off their intellectual capacity? This human trait is not obvious when you look upon someone for the first time. With many mental attributes possible, human intelligence can vary from person to person. The definition for human intelligence is: capacity for learning, reasoning, understanding, and similar forms of mental activity; aptitude in grasping truths, relationships, facts, and meanings. [15] The educational community has come to accept the various types of intelligence's or *Multiple Intelligences* as defined by the work of Howard Gardner, a developmental psychologist at Harvard University. According to Gardner, there are seven defined areas of human intelligence. They are:

- Linguistic intelligence involves sensitivity to spoken and written language, the ability to learn languages, and the capacity to use language to accomplish certain goals. This intelligence includes the ability to effectively use language to express oneself rhetorically or poetically; and language as a means to remember information. Writers, poets, lawyers and speakers are among those that Gardner sees as having high linguistic intelligence.

- Logical-mathematical intelligence consists of the capacity to analyze problems logically, carry out mathematical operations, and investigate issues scientifically. In Gardner's words, this entails the ability to detect patterns, reason deductively and think logically. This intelligence is most often associated with scientific and mathematical thinking.

- Musical intelligence involves skill in the performance, composition, and appreciation of musical patterns. It encompasses the capacity to recognize and compose

---

[15] intelligence. (n.d.). Online Etymology Dictionary. Retrieved December 31, 2012, from Dictionary.com website: http://dictionary.reference.com/browse/intelligence

musical pitches, tones, and rhythms. Musical intelligence runs in an almost structural parallel to linguistic intelligence.

- Bodily-kinesthetic intelligence entails the potential for using one's whole body or parts of the body to solve problems. It is the ability to use mental abilities to coordinate bodily movements. Gardner sees mental and physical activity as related.

- Spatial intelligence involves the potential to recognize and use the patterns of wide space and more confined areas.

- Interpersonal intelligence is concerned with the capacity to understand the intentions, motivations and desires of other people. It allows people to work effectively with others. Educators, salespeople, religious and political leaders and counselors all need a well-developed interpersonal intelligence.

- Intrapersonal intelligence entails the capacity to understand oneself, to appreciate one's feelings, fears and motivations. In Gardner's view, this involves having an effective working model of ourselves, and to be able to use such information to regulate our lives."[16]

Generally speaking, these attributes stem from either nature or nurture. They often work synergistically to bring out these attributes in a person. The nature contribution will stem from your genetic inheritance or your family lineage. Your mother, father, grandparents, and great-grandparents are the possible sources where these inherited capacities can originate. The nurturing contribution will be from the environmental factors, which promoted the development of already latent talents or from talent that has a sufficient

---

[16] Smith, Mark K. (2002, 2008) 'Howard Gardner and multiple intelligences', the encyclopedia of informal education, http://www.infed.org/thinkers/gardner.htm.

presence, for which the many factors can influence. Family, culture, and even societal expectations can cultivate the talent in question. This can eventually lead one to develop an exceptional mental attribute. So how will a person who has accentuated mental abilities be noticed? There are quite a few ways to be noticed for there are quite a few of these mental attributes. Each and every one type will also create a unique form of appeal for others to notice.

Different mental attributes will appeal to different people. This depends largely on what features a person possesses that will attract other people. Say you are an aspiring musician and you meet someone who has mastered a musical instrument that you have chosen to excel in. Would you not be impressed by this person who has excelled at and mastered this musical instrument? Would you not want to know more about this person on a personal level? Would you not want to learn how he/she has secretly mastered their skills? Say you are an art student who happens to meet a person who has recently significantly made a contribution to that particular form of art. Would you not be captivated by this person? Would you not make yourself available to listen to what that person has to say? Perhaps you see how a person can with great ease understand difficult mathematical or scientific concepts with little effort. Do you not become curious about how these individuals can achieve such mental feats? Do you not find yourself wanting to engage them and inquire on how they can accomplish such feats? Mental attributes can be just as powerful an attractive force as physical features. One simply has to be aware that they are being drawn to those individuals for these reasons.

A person with interpersonal intelligence, besides having masterful feats of intelligence, can also demonstrate other attributes as well. These individuals can also be suave, debonair, well-cultured, dashing, graceful in speech and behavior, elegant in appearance, and sophisticated. Who among us wouldn't be positively influenced by meeting such a person who can skillfully meet, entertain, and keep you enthralled by their presence? A person with evolved intrapersonal skills is likely to be self-aware, cognizant of their own motives, ambitions, and needs and driven to accomplish their goals. For most of us, meeting people like this leads us to feel such admiration for them for reaching such a level of self-awareness, something that we all wish to accomplish within ourselves. We would want them to share with us their secrets of how they came to be so self-aware. We would also find ourselves drawn towards them as well.

These are the qualities that intellectually gifted individuals possess that draw us into their presence. Although not immediately obvious at times to our senses, intellectual capacity offers a unique appeal. We are left in admiration and veneration of these individuals. This is why people with strong intellectual capacities are so alluring. However, there is one more level of human development which can attract us to others—a developed spiritual capacity.

People are capable of growing in many areas. One facet of human potential that is possible is that of a spiritual capacity. I expand on this subject in my book *MY DEEP Training: An Uncommon Guide Towards Spiritual Growth and General Well Being*. I do so by emphasizing the aspirations of the human experience to develop an inner spirit. This spirit potential resides within us all. This highest and greatest of all human potential will provide for us abilities tomorrow which cannot be rationalized outside the context of spiritual potential. Spirituality is a way of being. Although not obvious to our senses, our emotional state, or our mind, it is a powerful dormant ability residing within the structure of all of us. As we consider how we all have inherent intangible qualities such as emotions and intellect which cannot be physically detected by our senses, it is possible for there to exist yet another ability within the human condition which is not immediately apparent. This potential can be awakened so that we can reach our full potential. This ability must be coerced into being awakened while we occupy ourselves with our daily activities. There are many facets available such as religious practice, meditation, personal studies into religion, prayer, and self-reflection. Through these practices, the spirit that resides within us can be stirred into awakening and prodded to grow. As humans awaken this potential within, they begin to demonstrate qualities unique to living a life of spirituality, which can demonstrate traits that we can find very attractive as people.

A person who has sufficiently evolved their awakened spirit can create a form of attractiveness unique to human attributes. Some of the following are individual characteristics of these individuals: a personal belief in a higher power and a developed connectedness to this higher power, a well-developed concept of a unifying connectedness to all beings, a well-established patience, a perceived deeper meaning and purpose to life, an improved quality of life, an increased peace of mind, decreased stress, improved relationships with others, a desire to reach out to others, a willingness to give, and a desire to increase a greater good throughout society. These are some of the basic personal and social attributes that a spiritually developed individual may exhibit.

Spiritually developed people demonstrate a charisma that stands apart from physical, emotional, and mental attributes. Spiritually developed individuals are people who can at times create a peace and tranquility that can be sensed by others near them. These individuals resonate an alluring aura. This is a very appealing trait that has no equal among human qualities. These attributes are possible with spiritually matured individuals.

Through developing spiritual capacity, one can naturally develop an appeal unique among human attributes. It can be a powerfully alluring quality to an evolved person. This quality can bring one to a peaceful state being around spiritually developed individuals. Although a most unique characteristic to humans, spiritual development is one of the many qualities that can attract one human being to another.

People are always being noticed. Some people possess physical attributes that can create strong sexual appeal. Demonstrating optimal physical characteristics, these individuals attract us in part by our biological drive and in part due to them possessing certain physical attributes. This can be because of past experiences. Or it may simply be that these individuals demonstrate a quality that appeals to our personal preferences. Some people demonstrate an emotional appeal that in turn demonstrates characteristics of a calm, caring, loving individual who can make you comfortable to be around. Other individuals will show their intellectual attributes. These suave and refined individuals can show reasoning skills, musical abilities, enhanced self-awareness, and other refined abilities that most of us admire. These attributes are often highly sought out. Lastly, the spiritually developed individual resonates a unique quality. These individuals are appealing due to their enhanced state of being, having evolved a powerful inner potential and established a connection to a divine source. They can create a charismatic peace and the well-earned admiration of those around them. Of course, the attribute one is drawn to is largely dependent upon where one is in one's own level of personal growth.

Humans are thriving, learning, and growing beings. As we learn and grow in our own unique set of experiences and thought processes, we are naturally drawn to others to provide us assistance in reaching our goals. Through our needs to be constantly stimulated and experience new things, being in the company of a more diverse group of people provides a source of maximum stimulation and a reservoir of unique experiences. As we grow in our own capacity, we turn to others to guide us, accompany us, and at times to complete us. When we find a lifelong companion, we look forward living an entire lifetime with them simply because we resonate so well and bond deeply with this chosen individual. During our life's journeys, we seek out certain qualities in others to aid us in our individual growth. Whether they're behind us in growth, at our level, or ahead of us, others provide us those essential resources that can aid us in our own individual growth. We are drawn to people who demonstrate the qualities that we at times seek to find in ourselves. This is true whether these attributes are physical, emotional, mental, or spiritual in nature. Such are many of the reasons why we are drawn to others. Knowing who you are and what *you need* for yourself as you journey through the various stages of your life is an ideal situation. If you understand what needs lie within you that draws you to others, you can fulfill those needs that you require at that particular stage of your life. Be clear what you are seeking in others and what you are providing in return. When you have chosen your champion to assist you with your current needs, it may be prudent to have some foresight into what your future needs will also be so that you can anticipate these future needs from your chosen companion as well.

We are constantly learning, experiencing, and growing as individuals. We need others to grow along with us as we grow. We seek in our partner those qualities that can complete us and provide us with the essential components to continue our own growth and development. We are drawn to others in this process, be it for the physical, emotional, mental, or spiritual attributes they possess. Such is the nature of being human. Such are a most natural display of human behavior.

Life's Stages—How to Work with Them

This chapter will ask you to be more reflective. By assessing your past, present, and even future needs as they relate to your life's journey, you can begin to understand the nature of what you need in your life in order to help you understand your life's journey as it progresses forward in stages. By understanding these needs and stages in your life, you can better understand what has motivated you to seek out in others what you have sought out in yourself.

Psychologists tell us that from our past experiences we have become who we are today by the unique experiences we have encountered and how we responded. Our progress through life often hinges on how we react to the people, events, and circumstances in our lives. From this perspective, we seem to be intended to go through a series of stages and periods in life as the decades pass.

Psychologists inform us that we are destined to go through a series of stages as we live our lives. By understanding what we are expected to experience throughout these stages, we can come to understand where we are in this spectrum of anticipated experiences. All of his can add a level of comfort and predictability to our lives if we are willing to evaluate this type of information and use it to our favor. This predictability can prepare us to better meet those expected needs, which can allow us to develop healthier outcomes in our lives for ourselves and our companions. This concept is referred to as personality development in psychology. Let us explore these stages of human development to better grasp these expected stages.

Several psychologists have excelled in this area of human study. Two widely accepted theories in the stages of human development come from the following: Freud's psychosexual developmental stages and Erickson's psychosocial developmental stages. Let us begin our discussion of human development with the founding father of psycho-analysis—Sigmund Freud.

Sigmund Freud, who became a prominent figure in the early part of the 20th century for contributing to the concept of psycho-analysis, informed us that as children we were destined to demonstrate certain behaviors and go through certain stages. Freud tied in the concept of childhood experiences with parental rearing practices in relation to sexual patterns of behavior. Freud called these stages *psycho-sexual* developmental stages. These stages are as follow:

- Oral—Birth-1 year. The infant's ego (a concept Freud developed, in which the personality of the person is engaging with reality in real time) directs the baby's sucking activity towards breast or bottle. If needs such as the child's oral needs are not met appropriately, the infant may develop habits such as thumb sucking, fingernail biting, and pencil chewing in childhood as well as smoking and overeating in later life.

- Anal—1-3 years. Here toddlers and preschoolers enjoy holding and releasing urine and feces. Toilet training becomes a major issue between parent and child. If parents insist that children be trained before they are ready, of if they make too few demands, conflicts about anal control may appear in the form of extreme orderliness and cleanliness or messiness or disorder.

- Phallic—3-6 years. Here preschoolers take pleasure in genital stimulation, Freud's Oedipis conflict for boys and Electra conflict for girls arise, in which children feel a sexual drive for the opposite sex parent. To avoid punishment, they give up this desire and adopt the same-sex parent's characteristics and values. As a result, the Superego is formed (the moral and ethical aspect of the person that develops), and children feel guilty each time they violate its standards.

- Latency—6-11 years. Sexual instincts die down, and the superego develops further. The child acquires new social values from adults and same-sex peers outside the family.

- Genital—Adolescence. With puberty, the sexual impulses of the phallic stage reappear. If development has been successful during earlier stages, it leads to marriage, mature sexuality, and the birth and rearing of children. This stage extends through adulthood."[17]

From these early in life anticipated stages, Freud argued that the majority of personality development would be established mostly within the first decade of life. This was groundbreaking work approximately one hundred years ago. Through this concept of personality developmental theory, one can see the major conflicts that can arise between the sexes, along with the expected behavior patterns developed in a child's personality stemming from the first decade of life. Today, Freud's theory of personality development is considered controversial and outdated.

Another psychologist whose work in this field is still widely used to explain personality development is the work of Erik Erickson, who was a student of Freud. Erickson contributed further to the five stages of Freud's work by adding on more social interactions a person would have with other people throughout a person's lifespan while paying close attention to the parental influence factor. Erikson developed eight psychosocial stages. They are as follows:

- Basic trust versus mistrust—Birth-1 year. From warm, responsive care, infants gain a sense of trust, or confidence, that the world is good. Mistrust occurs when infants have to wait too long for comfort and are handled harshly.

---

[17] Berk, L. (2008). Exploring Lifespan Development. Allyn & Bacon Publishing. Boston, MA. 02116. Pg. 12.

- Autonomy versus shame and doubt—1-3 years. Using new mental and motor skills, children begin to choose and decide for themselves. Autonomy is fostered when parents permit reasonable free choice and do not force or shame the child.

- Initiative versus guilt—3-6 years. Through make-believe play, children explore the kind of person they can become. Initiative – which is a sense of ambition and responsibility – develops when parents support their child's new sense of purpose. When parents demand too much self-control, they induce excessive guilt.

- Industry versus inferiority—6-11 years. At school, children develop the capacity to work and cooperate with others. Inferiority develops when negative experiences at home, at school, or with peers lead to feelings of incompetence.

- Identity versus role confusion—Adolescence. The adolescent tries to answer the question, "who am I and what is my place in society?" By exploring values and vocational goals, the young person forms a personal identity. The negative outcomes are confusion about future adult roles.

- Intimacy versus isolation—Young adults work on establishing intimate ties to others. Because of earlier disappointments, some adults cannot form close relationships and remain isolated.

- Generativity versus stagnation—Middle adulthood. Middle-aged adults contribute to the next generation through child rearing, caring for other people, or productive work. The person who fails in these ways feels an absence of meaningful accomplishment.

- Ego integrity versus despair—late adulthood. Elders reflect on the kind of person they have been. Integrity results from feeling that life was worth living as it happened. Those who are dissatisfied with their lives fear death."[18]

Erikson's work on personality development was based both on parent-child interactions and major life events. One form by which Erikson developed his ideas was by observing young adults develop intimate ties to others as a more focused activity once they leave home to establish their own niche, was discovered to be a trend in the Intimacy versus Isolation stage. Expected life experiences within certain periods in one's life and the resolution of these conflicts were major factors in personality development according to these two theories. These were termed psychoanalytic theories of personality development. Other concepts of human development later emerged. They include Behaviorism, which states that directly observable events are the major contributing factors to human development. Social Learning Theory was another theory, in which conditioning principles such as constantly being pressured by the environment to behave in certain ways can produce new learned responses in people as a major contributing factor toward human development.

The many theories and concepts believed to contribute to human personality development are complex, and not one theory is accepted universally to explain the many facets of human development. However, through these developed theories one can see how life has predictable patterns. This predictability can provide insights into one's needs during the various stages of life.

Another concept which can provide insight into expected human need is the concept of Major Periods of Human Development. Berk (2008) would agree that life contains certain fixed periods.[19] Through these expected periods in life, we can see how we develop and what our

---

[18] Berk, L. (2008). Exploring Lifespan Development. Allyn & Bacon Publishing. Boston, MA. 02116. Pg. 13.
[19] Berk, L. (2008). Exploring Lifespan Development. Allyn & Bacon Publishing. Boston, MA. 02116. Pg. 7.

expected needs will be during certain phases of our lives. These periods are as follow:

- Prenatal—Conception to birth. The one-cell organism transforms into a human baby with remarkable capacities to adjust to life outside the womb.

- Infancy and toddlerhood—Birth-2 years. Dramatic changes in the body and brain support the emergence of a wide array of motor, perceptual, and intellectual capacities and first intimate ties to others.

- Early childhood—2-6 years. During the "play years," motor skills are refined, thought and language expand at an astounding pace, a sense of morality is evident, and children begin to establish ties to peers.

- Middle childhood—6-11 years. The school years are marked by advances in athletic abilities: logical thought processes; basic literacy skills; understanding of self, morality, and friendship; and peer-group membership.

- Adolescence—11-18 years. Puberty leads to an adult-sized body and sexual maturity. Thought becomes abstract and idealistic and academic achievement grows more serious. Adolescents work on defining personal values and goals and establishing autonomy from their family.

- Early adulthood—18-40 years. Most young people leave home, complete their education, and begin full-time work. Major concerns are developing a career, forming an intimate partnership; and marrying, rearing children, or establishing other lifestyles.

- Middle adulthood—40-65 years. Many people are at the height of their careers and obtain leadership positions. They must also help their children begin independent lives and their parents adapt to aging. They become more aware of their own mortality.

- Late adulthood—65 years-death. People adjust to retirement, decreased physical strength and health, and often to the death of a spouse. They reflect on the meaning of their lives."[20]

As can be seen by this general overview of expected periods in life, people generally tend to go through certain expected events and periods. Depending upon your current age, you will likely find yourself striving toward the indicated goals within your age group. These trends offer insights into what are expected basic needs. In the name of achieving these needs, we will tend to seek out others to help us fulfill those personal needs. Others will also seek us out for these same reasons, depending upon where they also are in their lives. What seems obvious as searching for a companion to complete a particular need to either be touched, not be alone, or simply wanting to experience physical pleasure can actually be masking another deeper motive that explains why we are drawn to another person. That true motive may be the human drive to complete certain requirements within a stage, as Freud and Erikson have theorized. There is also another viable explanation to explain why we are drawn to others—Maslow's Hierarchy of Needs.

Abraham Maslow was a humanistic psychologist (psychologist who emphasizes the positive aspects of human behavior), whose original work showed the positive qualities that people could potentially obtain once a certain set of step-wise progressive needs were met. He entitled his work: Maslow's Hierarchy of Needs. As a person would begin their lives, certain needs would arise in order to live in an increasing qualitative state. As basic continually escalating needs would be met, other more complex needs would arise to allow this person an opportunity to express deeper, complex, internal

[20] Berk, L. (2008). Exploring Lifespan Development. Allyn & Bacon Publishing. Boston, MA. 02116. Pg. 7.

needs. Having met all lower previous needs, a person would reach the pinnacle of self-expression, called self-actualization. This self-actualization would express itself with a person having found fulfillment or a sense of completeness in their lives. This concept of Maslow's Hierarchy of Needs is expressed below:[21]

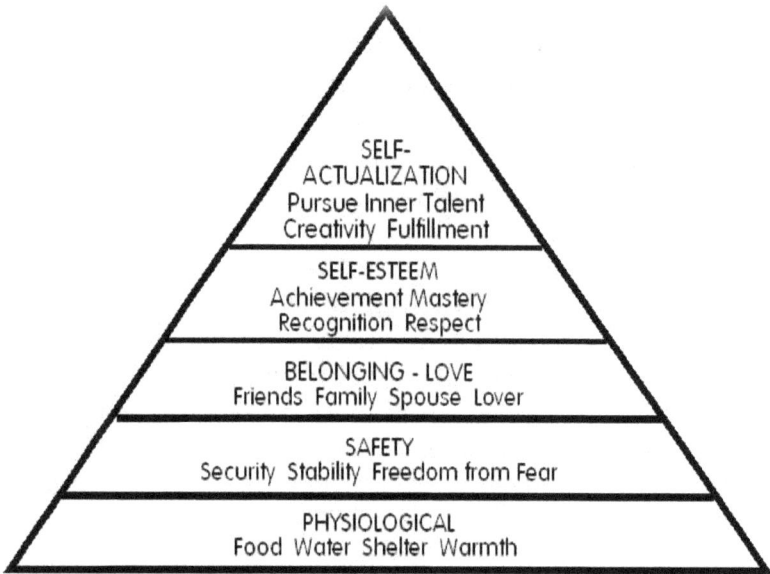

A pyramid requires a strong foundation in order to allow further growth up the structure. Once the foundational level is achieved, a progression of personal growth by the person having met essential progressively complex needs can be achieved. The foundation to this pyramid of needs, in order for any person to develop a higher state of qualitative living, is first meeting some basic essential needs. The pyramid

---

[21] McLeod, S. A. (2007). Maslow's Hierarchy of Needs. Image Retrieved from: http://www.simplypsychology.org/maslow.html

demonstrates that food, water, shelter, and warmth are some of those essential needs.[22] Other factors, such as breathing and sleep can also be added to this basic list. With these essential resources met on a continual basis, a person is ready for the next level of needs. The second level requirements in the pyramid are security, stability, and order to routine activities. Of one of these requirements such as stability can be focused on. Stability is required in many of life's activities. Without stability there can be no predictability and safety. The need for safety is essential in order for the person to be able to have predictability. Therefore, one need may support another need within the same pyramidal level. Once these next higher level needs are met, the person is ready to progress up the third level of needs. The third level requirements meet a powerful need of all human beings – the need to be touched. Here, the development of relationships and family structure can be achieved through the expression of affection and bonding. Having people in your life is fundamental to human activity. Humans are social beings and having people around you provides the resources for you to fulfill those needs. Of course, the quality – not the quantity – of your relationships with certain people provides the essential component to fulfilling the need of belongingness. Once this level of needs is fulfilled, the fourth level of needs surfaces. This fourth level is self-esteem. This is achievable through self-perseverance and interactions with others. It is the ability to develop self-esteem, which becomes an essential component to quality of life. Feeling good about your accomplishments, the realization of expressed self-potential, and personal growth are essential components to improving how one feels about oneself. Reaching goals generates a feeling like no other, which in turn generates greater self-esteem.

A person having fulfilled all or most previous needs, a powerful peak ability surfaces within the human experience—self-actualization. At this level, the person experiences something close to a spiritual experience. Seeking personal

---

[22] McLeod, S. A. (2007). Maslow's Hierarchy of Needs. Retrieved from http://www.simplypsychology.org/maslow.html

growth and unique experiences such as peak experiences (an example of this concept is when one is in the moment, fulfilled with what they are doing while engaged in this particular activity), the person expresses the pinnacle of their internal needs—to be fully expressed in the most inspirational highest form of self-expression. It is estimated that only about 2-3% of the population have experienced what can be considered a peak experience. This self-actualization level provides opportunity in one's life to complete the human experience while living by having evolved one or two or even three potent outlets of self-expression from the many possibilities of human potential. Maslow's psychological construct theory of human needs provides for us the ability to better understand some of our own clearer motives as to why we search others to connect with them. Others also turn to you to complete some aspect of their needs as well. This is a mutually rewarding behavior found within the human species.

Maslow's Hierarchy of Needs demonstrates a progressive human potential to grow and develop once certain needs are met. This is a form of a progressively escalating pattern. Interestingly enough, being offered warmth and affection, a need found midway through Maslow's pyramid, would not be as important if the person did not have food or water available which can be found at the lowest level of the pyramid. Compromising any needs from the base of this pyramid potentially compromises higher progressive needs. These higher needs in the pyramid could not be met if this were the case. These are the working components of Maslow's pyramid. In essence, we humans carry a strong internal drive to express and fulfill an escalation of needs so as to release a powerful inner potential. This inner potential can be achieved by meeting certain basic requirements, until a pinnacle of self-expression is reached. People who are considered fully self-expressed can exhibit certain behaviors.

An interesting point to be made here are some of the characteristics that people who achieve self-actualization can demonstrate. They typically:

- Perceive reality efficiently and can tolerate uncertainty.

- Accept themselves and others for what they are.

- Are spontaneous in thought and action.

- Are problem-centered (not self-centered).

- Have an unusual sense of humor.

- Are able to look at life objectively.

- Are highly creative.

- Are iconoclastic without being purposefully unconventional.

- Are concerned for the welfare of humanity.

- Are capable of deep appreciation of basic life-experience.

- Establish deep satisfying interpersonal relationships with a few people.

- Have peak experiences.

- Have the need for privacy.

- Have democratic attitudes.

- Strong moral/ethical standards.[23]

It is clear that people who demonstrate these characteristics of self-actualization can also take on the

[23] McLeod, S. A. (2007). Maslow's Hierarchy of Needs. Retrieved from http://www.simplypsychology.org/maslow.html

apparent appearance of demonstrating what can be considered to be spiritual attributes as well. I would speculate that these self-actualized individuals obtain a state of spirituality as unique as their own individuality.

Maslow's Hierarchy of Needs can overlap with Erikson's developmental stages of personality formation and Berk's Major Periods of Human Development. All of these concepts clearly demonstrate a pattern of structured sequential developments and some of the required needs to be met within oneself.

As we have reviewed the stages of human personality development and the need-based structure of human progression, we can see that certain patterns can be anticipated. Through these stages of experiences and needs, we are being continually pushed forward in life. Each person will have a unique set of circumstances, complementing each different type of life being lived. Nonetheless, these anticipated future events can be found manifested in each life being lived. We will turn to others for completing these stages, periods, and needs by searching in others what we seek to fulfill within ourselves. By unconsciously desiring certain needs, we will often turn to others through those qualities they exhibit, be they physical, emotional, mental, or spiritual attributes, to aid us in fulfilling those needs. This is another reason why we are drawn to others. Others will also turn to us to fulfill their needs as well. There are many examples of how we are driven to others to help us complete our needs.

One example can be found in Erikson's Hierarchy of personality development, in the Intimacy versus Isolation stage. In this stage, the young adult having separated themselves from their parents, will desire to connect to another person to forge long-lasting bonds with them. Another example would be the Middle Adulthood period in life. Here a person will want to achieve a high level of success in their careers. If this person is not successful, they may turn to another person who has accomplished such a task in an area that the first person attempted to achieve. Another example can easily be found in Maslow's pyramid. If a person is close to self-actualizing or seems to always fall short, they may be drawn to someone who they sense has self-actualized. They may be drawn to this person, seeing them as a mentor, to aid them on what they require to complete their journey. These are some of the reasons we are drawn to others.

You have been involved, and are currently involved, in relationships with others for many reasons. One reason may be the naturally progressive stages of development we are all progressing through. Another reason would be the needs that surface within you as certain foundational needs have been met. Through a constant interplay between the various types of needs, be they physical, emotional, mental or spiritual in nature, we will have turned to those around us to help us reach these powerful internal drives. Others will also want their needs met and will do so with us. Today, either in a current relationship, or back to the search-and-conquer mode of companionship, we are often driven by needs that seem to be both progressive and chronological. By being aware that we are going through this process, we can better understand our conscious and subconscious motives for why we seek a partner, friend, or even an acquaintance. We seek to become more connected to them, while in the process, we come to fulfill ourselves. And we fulfill our chosen partner in return. This is the gift that is accessible to us all by simply realizing that we are being compelled forward by obvious or not-so-obvious stages and needs. Perhaps taking some time to reflect on what stage of your life you are in and what your current needs are while in this stage of life can help you understand what some of your motives may be as you seek out to connect with others. Perhaps careful daily journaling of the dynamics of your current relationship can help make known the true reasons behind your actions and relationships and what you are seeking from them. This approach to self-discovery can purify your intentions by discovering what you seek from your partner, or others in your life, and what you search for in yourself. Then, by using the material in this chapter, you can begin to reflect on your progress within the developmental stages in relation to your personal needs. A clearer picture of your true needs may come into focus if you find that some of your current relationships are uncomfortable or unfulfilling.

On the other hand, being in relationships that are comfortable, mutual, and beneficial can present you with the deep fundamental needs you require.

The Mirror—Reflections of Your Past

Relationships are essential to human nature. They can define us, complete us, and they can also be used as a type of mirror to help us reflect on the journey we have taken through life thus far. In this chapter, we will continue reflecting on what type of relationships you have had to help you better understand how these past experiences can offer insights into your developed character. These past relationships can reveal more about who you were becoming in your past. This reflective mirror of past relationships can better help you understand how you have come to be who you are today. Reflection can provide you with insight, helping you see what your needs were then and what they are today. Considering where you were on your personal developmental level at one time, you can better understand why you were drawn to the people whom you were in relationships with back then. In this chapter, journaling is strongly encouraged. Journaling as a tool can help you see objectively patterns developing within you.

Human beings need other human beings. From a decision to connect to someone (either in person, or by indirect contact), three requirements must be met in order to satisfy the basic needs of a relationship. Both parties must know each other, know what each other's goals are in the interaction and what do they want from each other. Relationships can spring forth for many reasons. Some are by inheritance (family) while others are by proximity associations. Some happen through socializing (as with friends and companions), while others happen through business engagements, and others yet by community activities such as sports or religious activities etc. Most of us choose to engage with others based on the availability and proximity of ourselves to others. If you live in a rural setting, you are likely more limited to the number of people you meet. If you live in a large metropolis, you know that you will hardly see the same groups of people when you are out and about. Therefore, you can control the number of people you want to engage with based solely on the dynamics of the population around you. You can also have a great deal of control by simply choosing to live in a part of the world where you will find people like you or with shared interests.

Being in a relationship affects all parties involved. Taking the time to understand one another's needs and sharing of yourself and your experiences with another person stimulates the growth for the both of you. As a relationship begins, it can either continue to grow more, such as two people meeting at a social scene where they become willing to meet again at another time and place, or end as fast as it started such as two people sharing a casual conversation as they are waiting in a lobby somewhere.

There are many types of interpersonal relationships. One type is the events which occur between a man and a woman who choose to meet and develop a romantic relationship. This kind of interpersonal relationship is capable of going through a series of five stages, according to the work of George Levinger, a well-known psychologist. Levinger argues that a relationship may have similar patterns as in human lifespans, such as birth, maturation, and closure. Levinger's five-stage model of a relationship is as follows:[24]

---

[24]Author Unknown (2010). Maintenance of relationships. 5 Stage Model – George Levinger 1980.
http://www.integratedsociopsychology.net/Relationship_Maintenance/5-stagemodel-GeorgeLevinger1980.html

A Acquaintance	Relationship starts with mutual attraction
B Build-up	Couple engage in self-disclosure and become increasingly interdependent
C Continuation	Couple's lives become enmeshed and the relationship becomes consolidated
D Deterioration	Relationship may deteriorate due to an imbalance of costs and rewards, or a high number of risk factors
E Ending	Deterioration may lead the couple to end the relationship

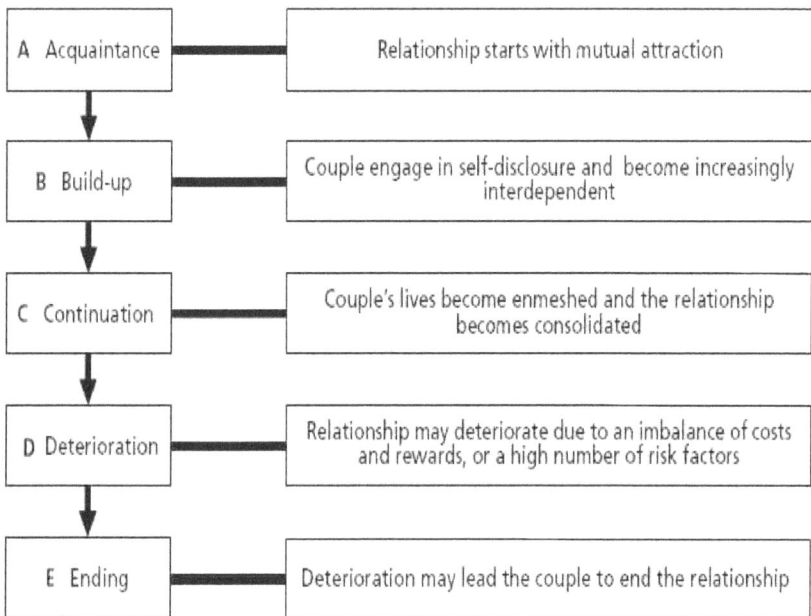

- Stage 1–Acquaintance. During the acquaintance stage, both individuals are attracted to each other either due to physical, emotional, mental and spiritual attributes. The new couple must be able to spend time together to get to know each other better. Lastly, both parties must be willing to take the relationship further.

- Stage 2–The Build-up Stage. During this stage, the relationship begins to take on a life of its own. Each individual grows more comfortable with intimacy and disclosure. Strong feelings develop for the other person during this phase. The compatibility of needs and desires will be a strong influence to keeping the couple together.

- Stage 3–Continuation Stage. This stage is marked by longevity in a relationship. Here, the relationship can go from months to years or even decades. This stage is often marked by becoming engaged to be married. Each person must be honest and trusting for the relationship to last.

- Stage 4—Deterioration. During this phase, the relationship begins to dissolve. Many of the fundamental structures to the relationship can begin to erode, such as a lack of trust, respect, and a loss of love. With the eventual outcome becoming clear, one or both parties will bring the relationship to an end.

- Stage 5–The Termination Stage. The relationship usually comes to an end, resulting in either separation (if both parties were not married) or divorce (if they were married). "[25]

These naturally occurring stages can be found through the many phases of one's life, from the initial puppy love early in life to a painful separation and divorce.

Today, we can easily reflect on our past relationships and see how we have grown from them. We were drawn to these people in the past. As Levinger's stage one indicates, we decided to pursue our engagements with that significant other of our past. Also, as Maslow's Hierarchy of Needs demonstrates, we were in the process of being driven to fulfill certain needs as we desired to evolve into more complex and sophisticated people. I would offer that we were in a process of developing multiple potentials within our being simultaneously. Our emotional and mental attributes may have been evolving, which produced needs at multiple levels at once. These needs required us to turn to others to help us

---

[25] http://www.managementstudyguide.com/stages-in-interpersonal-relationships.htm

develop these burgeoning attributes, which began to evolve within us.

A human being has several potential qualities: physical development of the body, emotional states of being, mental capacities, and spiritual growth. These attributes are always maturing, with certain attributes being more emphasized than others, depending on the developmental stage one is currently developing. I would suggest that the major stages in one's life can evolve in a synchronized chronological order. The physical aspect to the human potential can evolve relatively early in life. For example, by our early twenties, our physical bodies have completely evolved. There will be no addition of growth of the body, strength (unless athletic training is used), stamina, or speed (again, unless athletic training is used), etc. Emotional maturity may occur before the early thirties for women and perhaps even for men. If you are well into your mid-to late-forties, you can reflect on when you felt you reached the point where you were comfortable and capable of controlling your emotions and using your emotional strengths as an attribute in your life. It was likely during your early to mid-thirties. If you have not yet reached this age, you can inquire of your family, friends, and acquaintances, and ask them when they felt they had reached their emotional maturity.

The next attribute that can reach maturity is one's optimal mental abilities. It is well-known that during our forties, the human brain begins to reach an optimal neuronal white matter transmitting connectedness. This optimal connectedness of connections between neurons allows the brain to transmit neuronal signals and thus evolve the frontal lobe of the brain to reach their maximal state of processing and connections. The frontal lobe is essential for abstract thinking and reasoning. Thus, many of the universities and colleges are filled with male and female professors who are teaching complex subjects in the classroom. Many of these men and women are in their forties and beyond. Lastly, the spiritual capacity of a person is a bit more complex. The spiritual capacity of a person seems to have great potential and endless growth capacity. If true, a human lifetime is not a sufficient amount of time to fully mature our inner spirit which dwells within the framework of a human being. Only a few religious leaders of the past have evolved their spirits sufficiently enough to demonstrate that during their lifetime they had succeeded in maturing their spirit.

We are always in the process of evolving our body, our emotional state, our mind and our spirit. Our age, experiences, inner drives, and the people we are connected to, all contribute to this process. Erikson mentions that we are always in progressive stages. I would add that we have also been working toward developing all four of these attributes previously mentioned. For example, by the time we have a well-developed physical body, most men and women will also have contributed to maturing their emotional state. Of course the mind also will have matured considerably in one's mid-twenties as compared to adolescence. As we strive for personal development, we learn that we needed others to help us grow and mature. Let us now examine how relationships are such an essential part of our growth.

As mentioned in the first chapter, the foundation of our ability to develop relationships stem from our first years with our parents. The interactions our parents provided us and our responses to them helped program us into developing a lifetime strategy to engage others. Our early years would pass and we were of sufficient age to become aware of our emotions and thoughts. We began to explore them by experiencing life in its great abundance of novelty experiences. Life seemed more fulfilling when you were engaging others near you. The first relationships apart from your family and neighborhood acquaintances may have been those of your classmates. An extensive opportunity to engage others provided itself through school. So, as we recall, our first *puppy love* brought to our awareness unknown emotions, such as a euphoria sensation and a rapid heart rate. Never to revert back to a previous non-awakened state of emotional dormancy, we all went forth in exploring this newfound ability to be so alive and awakened by someone else. Since then, we have experienced a continual cycle of relationships. Through these relationships we have been provided many of the needs, wants, desires, drives that allow growth and maturation. So which was your first serious relationship and what did it provide for you?

For most of us, our first serious relationship was probably the one where you considered being with that person for your entire life. How old were you when this happened? Perhaps your late teens or early twenties? According to Erikson's stages of development, you were either in your Identity versus Role confusion or your Intimacy versus Isolation stage. I would argue that you also were maturing much of your physical and emotional drives through this first powerful relationship. So why did you feel that this person was the person you wanted to be with all your life? Did you enjoy how alive you felt when you were around this person? Did you enjoy the excitement and novelty you experienced while being around them? Of course. These first relationships demonstrated that you wanted to connect and be in the moment with that one person. However, there is more to why you may have wanted to connect to that person.

As we travel through adolescence, we have to go through many painful experiences. We must develop confidence as to who we are and what we are becoming. We must be accepted by our peers. We must learn to slowly sever the powerful dependence we have with our parents. We must focus on developing our talents. We must explore our interests. We must continue to maintain ties with our nucleus family and relatives. We must fight negative thoughts and emotions, such as being rejected by friends and peers. These previously mentioned interactions can often discourages us from accepting ourselves. Still, we must begin to accept the fact that we will have limitations in our lives. We may not be the most popular, influential, or intelligent person in our circle of friends. We must learn that school is not only a place where you must be, but also a place where opportunities will be provided in the years to come. We must learn that rules and laws are placed in our society for a reason. We must also become aware that there are many opportunities to develop powerful relationships with so many other people.

There are countless other lessons that we must learn during our adolescence. Many of these lessons bring conflict, strife, confusion, doubt, and disbelief with them. At times, we will turn to others to comfort us. We will want them to provide clarity to us about what we are experiencing at times. We turn to others not only to feel alive and experience novelty, but also for comfort and advice. This is a natural and healthy outlet. So who were you becoming and what were you going through when you entered into the first few relationships?

Reflect for a moment on your the first intense relationship. Why were you drawn to that person? What were your needs at that time? What did you learn from them? Why did you leave? Taking the time to reflect on what you gained from being with someone will reveal what your needs and intentions were at that time. A possible strong reason was that they demonstrated the capacity to fulfill some of your needs at that time. Of course, you were more than eager to explore their needs along with your experiences with them. These were mutually beneficial encounters. So reflecting back once again, what were you going through that drew you to that person? Which relationship was most satisfying to you? Why was it so satisfying to you? Did this person provide for you your emotional needs, physical needs, mental needs or a combination of these needs? Did this person give to you the experience of fully connect to someone so as to complete yourself at that time? Let us also discuss those less than desirable relationships of the past.

We can all recall being in a relationship where we kept asking ourselves "Why am I with this person? These people whom we shared these experiences with, we thought were fulfilling our needs but perhaps did not fulfill the more healthy set of needs we had at that time. Being in relationships where you or your partner demonstrated unacceptable social behaviors such as breaking the law or being in either a physical, emotional, or mentally abusive relationship was not a comfortable experience. Perhaps you chose to be with that person because an internal conflict did not resolve itself and you found yourself needing to vent. Did you enter into this type of relationship to help you de-stress your thoughts and feelings? If this was not the issue, then what was so appealing about them? Was it their confidence or their rebellious nature?

Perhaps you chose a partner who was unfaithful. Perhaps you stayed with them anyway? If so, what fulfilled this need to continue to stay with them even though they were compromising your self-esteem or confidence? Did you develop a co-dependency with them? What needs were being fulfilled from these past experiences?

With so many negative interactions possible, being in these types of experiences quickly taught many of us that we wished to end them. These experiences provided great contrast to what we considered to be pleasant and unpleasant experiences. They also provided clarity for what you needed and what you didn't need. Perhaps we stayed in these relationships for an extended period of time even though we knew better. Perhaps, in reflecting on what happened in the past, we have learned what we want and what we do not want in dealing with others. If we find ourselves today scarred from these past negative interactions, perhaps we are ready today to receive some guidance in the form of a counselor or therapist to aid us in our search to better understand ourselves.

Taking time to reflect on your past experiences and considering the stages, needs, wants, and drives of the human condition, we can learn powerful insights into who we were becoming. These past reflections also tell us how we became the person we are today. We are all still in the process of growing. We are still in the process of developing our emotional, mental, and spiritual potential. We are still in the process of coming to a state of balance with these constant needs so as to full express ourselves fully, as Maslow has so eloquently pointed out.

So how are your relationships going today? Perhaps you are seeking someone new? Perhaps you have been in long-term relationship for some time. Knowing what your needs have been, what experiences you have had, and reflecting on how past relationships have shaped you, it's possible to better understand who you are today. You still have needs and you are constantly evolving. Your emotional, mental, and spiritual abilities are still being shaped, even today. If you are currently in a long-term relationship, your needs have been and are likely currently being met. Raising children and having a supportive, loving, and giving companion in a relationship are great treasures. You are growing in ways that you did not know you could along your path to self-discovery. If you have recently entered into a relationship, or if you are seeking a relationship today, keep in mind that you are maturing and evolving based on a continuum of needs. By being aware of your physical, emotional, mental, and spiritual needs, and being cognizant of your level of growth or stage in life you are in, you can more clearly see what you are looking for in a relationship. This is a great approach to entering into a new relationship. This is how you can become more successful with your current relationship or with a new relationship.

Entering into relationships is a never-ending human endeavor. Relationships, as Levinger presented, begin, mature, and *perhaps* cease over time. Through this human need comes the opportunity to grow, mature, and evolve. By reflecting on the past, you can come to understand why you entered into relationships, how you have grown from them, and in which direction of growth you are currently heading. We can also, by reflecting on the future stages of life, see what your needs will be as well as where you are headed towards. Such is the nature of the mirror of reflection.

Completing the Full Image—Where to now?

This final chapter will bring together concepts presented in previous chapters. By now, we have looked into our past and reflected within to better grasp what more accurate description the mirror can provide us. Through these discoveries, we can see who stands before the mirror today. What do you bring forth and offer your chosen companion? Hopefully, these self-reflective exercises have helped the answer become more apparent. This was the goal of reading this material thus far.

Looking back, it's obvious that this journey of self-reflection to the present state of self-awareness has been an arduous one. We began by looking back on the foundations of how we first structured relationship building. This was accomplished by thinking about the relationships you developed from your engagements with your mother and father. What did you discover from this exercise? Did you discover that the relationship you had with your mother molded your approach to building relationships? Did you feel the world was a safer place because of your loving and caring mother's influence upon you as a child, which led to higher levels of trust? As a woman, did you find yourself acting like your mother, as she had interacted with your father, when you would engage other potential partners? Perhaps being a girl in conflict with your mother, did you see perhaps a pattern of engaging other women in your past in a negative form, and found yourself having more male friends instead? There are many possibilities and outcomes that are made concrete through this stage of your development.

As a man, do you see yourself becoming your father when you engage women today, just as your father interacted with your mother? To what degree do you catch yourself mimicking your father's phrases and behaviors with women? In what manner did your father show his respect for your mother? Do you show the same form of respect for women now or do you do something different today? What about your siblings?

How are your relationships with your peers? Are you comfortable with the level of closeness you have with your acquaintances or work associates? What about your friends? Do you feel satisfied with how you engage your friends or do you find yourself constantly replacing your friends for people who no longer seek your company? There are many outcomes possible with your first primary relationships. Recognition of this fact is essential in the process of self-discovery. Family, however, is not the only contributor to personal experiences in developing a strategy for relationship building.

Although your first family relationships were fundamental to your development, other environmental factors such as nationality, culture, race, family traditions, and even gender identity also contribute greatly after your 3rd to 5th year of life. For example, being born in the United States would be a different experience of engaging the opposite sex than it would be in another country. The acceptable boundaries of engaging the opposite sex is dictated strongly by the dominating culture found in that country. Each country has its traditions and family values along with an established culture. This in turn affects the national values that prevail within that country. From the liberal cultural approaches of the United States and Europe, to the conservative standards of the Middle East, to the deeply rich traditional influences found in China and Japan, all areas of the world would have shaped you greatly in the method and approach by which you understood how to engage members of the opposite sex.

So how cognizant are your of cultural influences? This is a very difficult determination to make. One of the best ways to identify how your surroundings have shaped your ideas and concepts about socializing with the opposite sex is by being exposed to other cultures and nationalities. For those who have traveled abroad, it is easy to see how other cultures and people differ from your way of life. Seeing how others live can reveal how easy it is to identify when observing their behaviors and entering into discussions in which thoughts and ideas are being exchanged just how different they are from you. When provided with this profound insight into how your society has shaped you, by studying other cultures and people, it's easier to accept the differences between people of different cultures. Through this open-minded perspective, it's clear that no one way of life is better than others. However, when you attempt to understand how you have become the person you have become from your environmental settings, it is quite surprising to see how you could be different if you had been raised in another culture. So can you be objective in understanding how your national culture, traditions, race, and even gender experiences has shaped your concept of how you approach your significant other? Perhaps, taking the time to reflect on how acquaintances from other cultures approach their relationships can provide some contrast to how you approach your relationships with the opposite sex. Through this comparative insight, you can see if you will need to improve, slightly adjust, or maintain your strategies for seeking and prolonging your chosen relationship.

Another point to consider is how we have been influenced today to accept our gender identity. This also strongly influences how we engage the opposite sex, which stems from our powerful need to reproduce – our biological drive. It is clear that we have a strong reproductive drive. Coursing through our blood vessels can be found the powerful chemical hormones, testosterone and estrogen. These hormones help adapt our bodies, preparing us to create children and providing the psychological drive to advertise and pursue our chosen partner. This ingrained reproductive drive to procreate alerts our everyday thinking, reminding us to be vigilant toward this demanding course of action for most of our young adult and middle-aged lives. From the biologically created primary sexual characteristics that people have (men and women's unique set of genitals) and secondary sexual characteristics specific to our gender (men having a larger stature, and greater upper body strength, while women have larger hips and breasts), these differences have provided within our bodies, the resources to build and distinguish our gender identities. Of course the chromosome patterning of each sex as well as the hormones flowing through the blood of each gender was the building block for the gender's to begin the process of building one's gender identity as well. Thus, a man is a man due to his genetic inheritance and his hormonal influences. A woman is a woman as well for these same reasons. These influences also shape the way we desire to engage the opposite sex. Men are well known to be the aggressors while women are often known to be pacifists. Hence, it seems like an inescapable fact that we have been greatly influenced by our gender identity. Through this developed identity, we compare ourselves to others and seek out what we find attractive in others.

Being attracted to the opposite sex is possible through one of many preferences. The physical presentation of a potential partner is one of the first biological signals that draw us towards a potential mate. Demonstrating to the opposite sex the physical traits you possess is really the process of demonstrating the genetic material you have available to procreate. Through the reproductive drive, you demonstrate your secondary sexual characteristics to the opposite sex. By advertising your physical features, you are signaling to any potential mate your level of capability and readiness to reproduce. These powerful signals attract potential partners. You are also in search of a potential companion. Of course, once you have been drawn in by a potential mate through the ritual of courtship, you can further assess the compatibility of your new partner by engaging them at different levels such as an emotional or mental level. More evolved individuals will also be looking for a spiritual compatibility from their mate.

Emotionally evolved individuals will demonstrate a level of emotional composure. They will be able to use their mastered emotions to their benefits by making you more comfortable with your emotions. The mentally endowed individual will attract others based on their level of skill and shared interests. Many individuals are drawn in by these admirable traits. The confidence they demonstrate to the world draws you in as well, for example. The spiritually endowed individual will resonate an energy of peace and tranquility, affecting people around them. Depending upon the level of personal development you find yourself currently in, you may find yourself seeking out the type of person that demonstrates the physical, emotional, mental, or spiritual aptitude you desire. These are the types of influences an individual may possess that can draw you into their company. Depending on what you find attractive, you may want to get to know certain individuals possessing these qualities and even begin building a relationship with them. Being aware that we are drawn in by these factors can empower us to become conscious of what we seek, and more importantly, what we need from a relationship. Lastly, we can also learn from ourselves by looking back into our own past relationships.

We all have a past. Our prior relationships are an inseparable part of our pasts. Looking back on them can provide insight into how we came to be who we are today. Our past relationships offer us a window to see ourselves objectively. Reflecting on previous relationships, it's important to consider what we learned from them. More importantly, why were you in these past relationships? What did you need from these individuals at the time? Also, what drew you to them? Being able to answer some of these questions sincerely can act as a guide to steer you where you want to be in your present. So what do these facts of your past tell you? What were your needs at that time? Perhaps, in your youth, you simply wanted to discover more about yourself by being around others who allowed you to express yourself more. Perhaps you were curious about the opposite sex and simply wanted to explore what you would find about them. Maybe you wanted to feel free from responsibility and sought out adventure, finding a companion with similar interests along the way. Perhaps you found a very interesting person you were drawn to. There were likely many reasons, during your early years, why you reached out to others. Finding what motivated you is the key to understanding your past.

During your early twenties, perhaps you felt the need to start a family or perhaps you desired to travel abroad? Settling in with someone in a long-term relationship might have comforted you. Perhaps you were simply lonely, being away from your family for the first time. Maybe you were focused on making money or continuing with higher education and needed someone there to cushion the stress in your life. Whatever the reason, you reached out to someone and connected with them at some level. You understood that you simply needed to bond, as you had bonded many times in your past. These wonderful years of youthful energy, with so many opportunities to explore yourself and the world are not to be forgotten.

It is possible that your thirties were times of a more industrial nature? Why did you choose to settle down during this time? Are you still in this relationship? Do you still find that drive to be there? These are to be the difficult years with both family obligations and your career demanding your attention. Still, we continue to traverse through these years with much success.

Your mid-forties, fifties, and beyond are the decades where you are slowly stripped of your youthfulness. With this rite of passage comes understanding and wisdom. Your needs will change once again during this transition in your life. If you find yourself alone during this time, you will become more self-aware and gain a better understanding your personal needs. You may yet find yourself seeking out a partner who will provide a more compatible fit. Of course, these stages in your life align with Erikson's stages of development and Berk's chronological phases. Combining these concepts with Maslow's hierarchy of needs, we can have some predictability into what our needs will be once we reach each stage. Being aware of these phases can help us become aware of what motivates us to be drawn into a relationship and what we are seeking from a partner. As we evolve, we mature into people that we did not know existed within us. It is through this growth that we seek out others to accompany us. We find ourselves being drawn to them, and they being drawn to us. Companionship is as fundamental as breathing. It is an absolute requirement to some extent.

Without human company, we would not be able to develop our emotional and mental skills. Without human intervention, we would not be provided a resource to help our individual growth. We would also not have an outlet for self-expression nor a method to assist ourselves with our individual needs. We are human; therefore we need humanity. It is through our various complex relationships and interactions that we are able to continue on with this incredibly enjoyable and challenging journey that is life.

I speak of the many varied potentials within the human framework in my book; *MY DEEP Training: An Uncommon Guide Towards Spiritual Growth and General Well Being*. The book can be found in my website at *mydeept.com* as well if you are further interested in reading an inspirational, spiritual, self-help book.

I have concluded Part One of this book, which was aimed at preparing you for entering a relationship and self-reflection for those currently in a relationship. The aim was to be clear about the person you have become, so as to be certain what you presently offer your partner or your future potential partner. I hope that this material helped you engage in self-reflection, journaling, and taking time to process insights and facts that you gained about yourself. Through this process, I hope that you have gained powerful new insights into how you have come to be the person you are and what your current needs are today. This will help you become clear about what you require in a relationship, and what you can offer your partner. Of course, if you feel that many issues have been brought to the surface that you are not comfortable dealing with these issues alone, please feel free to seek out a counselor or therapist. These skilled individuals are highly qualified in helping you sort out many issues you have become aware of.

This book is soon to be followed by a second book. This second book will focus on how to develop a more dynamic relationship with your significant other. The book will offer many ideas on how to strengthen and mature your current relationship or future relationships with your chosen partner. The book will also guide those not currently in a relationship on how to be clear about what you need in a relationship, how to acquire it, and how to sustain it. The focus on the second book will be how to maintain a dynamic, thriving relationship. It is my hope that you will find much value in your search to self-discovery. Through the lessons learned from reflecting on these ideas, you can discover the beautiful person residing within you who deserves to be the most happiest person alive today! Should you have any questions for the author about material in this text, please feel free to contact me at my website at: *mydeept.com*. I look forward to hearing from you. Best wishes in your endeavors.

www.ingramcontent.com/pod-product-compliance
Lightning Source LLC
Chambersburg PA
CBHW070527030426
42337CB00016B/2136